I0427821

SUMMARY

This monograph was presented at the Strategic Studies Institute (SSI)-Carnegie Council conference connected with the Council's U.S. Global Engagement Program. In this case, the engagement in question is with Russia, and this monograph specifically addressed the issues of how those aspects of the reset policy with Moscow that concern arms control and proliferation are proceeding. It duly addresses the question of whether further reductions in strategic offensive weapons are likely anytime soon, i.e., is it possible to go beyond the parameters in the recently signed and so-called New Strategic Arms Reduction Treaty (START) treaty with respect to reductions. Other critical issues involve the issues of missile defenses that Moscow vehemently opposes and the question of tactical or nonstrategic nuclear weapons, which the North Atlantic Treaty Organization (NATO) wishes to have Russia reduce.

Therefore, this analysis delves deeply into Russia's strategic posture with regard to the questions of why it needs and prioritizes nuclear weapons and what it thinks about the necessity for retaining large numbers of them (relatively speaking) to meet the security challenges posed not only by the United States and NATO, but also China. Based on this analysis, which takes into account the asymmetries in force structures and in strategic orientations of the two or three main actors, the author argues that the United States, NATO, and Russia will find it difficult to move forward on these issues quickly and achieve large-scale nuclear reductions or strategic harmony in the foreseeable future.

At the same time, a key component of the reset policy is to obtain Russian assistance in stopping, if

i

not reversing, Iranian and North Korean proliferation. Here, it appears that the reset policy has reached the limit of its utility, for Russia maintains a highly ambivalent and ambiguous policy with respect to Iran. As a result, we are possibly reaching a political dead end regarding Iran. Meanwhile, the Six-Party Talks on North Korea have reached an impasse.

This monograph analyzes Russia's posture on these issues and suggests alternative courses of action for the United States to undertake with regard to Russia in order to advance U.S. goals, particularly with respect to the Korean issue. The approaches suggested by the author regarding the impasse over Korea place this issue in a broader regional setting and take into account the fact that this issue is fully implicated in and involves the fast-changing dynamics of the overall international situation in Northeast Asia, e.g., the Rise of China and Russo-Chinese partnership there. It suggests far-reaching and innovative measures for the United States to take that would possibly break the logjam over Korea, but also would enable the United States to uphold a viable strategic equilibrium in Northeast Asia under conditions of dramatic change there.

ARMS CONTROL AND PROLIFERATION CHALLENGES TO THE RESET POLICY

INTRODUCTION

The so-called New Start Treaty between Russia and the United States entered into force in February 2011. Consequently, this treaty constitutes a baseline for all future bilateral, if not multilateral, efforts at arms control and nonproliferation involving these two powers, including President Barack Obama's long-term commitment to reaching nuclear zero. Moreover, due to the saliency of the issues of tactical nuclear weapons (TNW) and missile defenses in any future negotiation, this treaty possesses great importance for the future architecture of European security as well. The same holds true as Russia and the United States reduce their nuclear arsenals in the context of China's unceasing rise in military power that causes anxiety for both these states. Therefore, the treaty and subsequent arms control developments will possess considerable or even greater significance for Asian security, especially from Russia's standpoint.[1]

Finally, this treaty is the most important and impressive manifestation of what the two governments view as the success of the Obama administration's reset policy since 2009. Certainly, it is the most tangible expression of bilateral cooperation under that policy framework. So if something happened to the treaty and the new regime it postulates, the reset policy would likely fall apart. Yet, despite its importance, the success of the reset policy, and of future bilateral or multilateral accords on arms control and nonproliferation, is by no means guaranteed. Indeed, one thing both sides, as well as external observers, agree about is the very fragility of the reset policy.[2] And it is quite likely that if this policy were to falter, it would also diminish chances for further reductions in strategic arsenals among all nuclear powers, not just Russia and the United States. Thus the reasons for this fragility and the consequences for arms control and future cooperation on nonproliferation issues must be clarified.

There are many reasons for this fragility. Already by February 2011, discordant notes on European security were being heard in the European-Russian dialogue, a large part of whose current agenda is connected to issues of missile defenses and TNW, indicating substantive differences of outlook on key questions and continuing mutual mistrust.[3] Moreover, Russian governmental figures like Foreign Minister Sergei Lavrov now say that the the test of Russian relations with the North Atlantic Treaty Organization (NATO) and of NATO's "sincerity" is progress towards creating a joint missile defense system on Russia's terms.[4] This posture is analogous to Moscow's similar statements that the success of the new treaty depends on the United States not building its missile defense system, for Russia has already formally stated that such construction, if it continues, represents grounds for withdrawal from the treaty. Some may believe that these positions are merely negotiating tactics. But they also suggest a continuing Russian resort to the Soviet tactic of endless demands based on a sense that Moscow can keep pushing at no cost to divide NATO and induce Western concessions, while also attempting to browbeat or intimidate the West into concessions. They also suggest Moscow's continuing obsession with being able to intimidate Europe with the unimpeded threat of nuclear strikes against key European targets and its linked belief in the possiblity of using nuclear weapons in a warfighting role, however circumscribed that role might be. Nevertheless, Russia's positions on these particular issues are hardly the only reasons for concern over the fragility of the reset policy, arms control, and progress on nonproliferation.

Beyond those policy differences and the long-standing mutual suspicion between Moscow and the West as a whole (not just Washington), there exist substantial domestic constituencies in both the United States and Russia who are still driven by fundamental mistrust of each other. While those parties could not stop ratification of the treaty, major strategic issues still divide Russia and the United States as much as they unite them. For example, 39 Republican Senators cautioned the Obama administration about allowing Russia undue influence over the U.S. (and NATO) missile defense program.[5] And Republican Senate leaders are now attempting to force the administration to lock in $85 billion for nuclear modernization programs.[6] One could easily find analogous constituencies in Russian politics.

What drives these state-to-state, or NATO-Russia, and intrastate domestic struggles are deep-rooted fears of each other, as well as continuing regional rivalries. Apart from the fate of arms control in the future, the potential for major regional rivalries in Eurasia, or unforeseen events like the NATO air operation against Libya that began in March 2011, have the potential to undermine, disrupt, and even possibly rupture the reset relationship. Apart from consideration of trends in arms control policy, we must remember Abraham Lincoln's observation that "I claim not to have controlled events, but confess plainly that events have controlled me." Thus issues unrelated to the arms control agenda

3

can seriously compromise the capability of both Russia and the United States to move forward on that agenda as happened in 2001-09 and before that in the 1970s and 1990s. Indeed, it has generally been the case that while Moscow and Washington have been able to find agreement on issues of bilateral arms control, previous efforts at détente in the 1970s, 1990s, and 2001-09 have faltered largely due to rivalries over regional security questions in Eurasia. Today because so many of those issues remain unresolved and new ones like the NATO operation in Libya frequently crop up on the international agenda, the potential for discord remains strong.

This is especially the case as major bilateral disputes over missile defenses, TNW, and Eurasian security have only been temporarily suppressed but not resolved, while both sides' gains from the reset are of dubious durability. Furthermore, as Libya shows, Russia remains unwilling to accept the bottom line of U.S. national security policy, i.e., American leadership and (the intermittent) promotion of a global democratic order (which Russia regards as efforts at a unilateralist hegemony).[7] Likewise, the gains for the United States may not be lasting either. As of this writing, there is no sign of lasting progress in Afghanistan, even though the United States killed Osama Bin Laden on May 2, 2011 (local time), and U.S. plans for remaining there after 2014 already arouse Russian suspicions.[8] Moreover, both Iranian and North Korean proliferation continue unabated, calling into question the profitability and sustainability for the United States of the reset policy.

RUSSIA'S AMERICAN OBSESSION

Meanwhile, in Russia's case it is even fair to call its fears about U.S. power, policies, and proclivities obsessions concerning U.S. objectives. Russian journalist Leonid Radzikhovsky has said, "The existential void of our politics has been filled entirely by anti-Americanism" and that to renounce this rhetoric "would be tantamount to destroying the foundations of the state ideology."[9] Similarly, Fedor Lukyanov, Editor of Russia in Global Affairs, writes that:

> The mentality of Russian politics is such that relations with the United States remain at the center of universal attention and virtually any problems are seen though an American prism. This is partially a reflection of inertia of thinking which is finding it hard to break with perceptions of Cold War times. It is partially a demonstration of a hidden desire to have a sense of our own significance. There is still a desire to compare ourselves specifically with the only superpower.[10]

Lukyanov also notes that both the United States and Russia see the other as being a power in decline.[11] And at least one Russian writer boasts that Russia bears primary responsibility for frustrating American unilateralism by shaping blocking coalitions that restrained and ultimately foiled U.S. designs.[12] Such thinking validates the contention by Kari Roberts, a Canadian scholar, that, "It appears as though the common themes in Russian foreign policymaking continue to be how Russia views itself vis-à-vis the U.S. and its pragmatic approach to identifying and tackling foreign policy problems."[13] For example, there is good reason to see Russia's Iranian policy as being closely tied to its perceptions of U.S. policies.

Concurrently, in Russia (if not the United States) issues connected to nuclear weapons make for major manifestations of political theater, and in both countries these issues are utilized for scoring points for or against parties in power regardless of the truth.[14] In the Russian case, this appears not just in overt and covert domestic political struggles, but also in the widespread, ingrained, and wholly unsubstantiated conclusion that the United States is essentially Russia's enemy and trying to suppress it, if not break it up, and that U.S. politics, like Russian politics, is essentially a matter of dictating to smaller powers and endless conspiracies, either mainly against Russia or within the U.S. Government. After all, that is the elite's own experience of Russian politics. And this habit of Russian projection of domestic phenomena and values onto the "other," i.e., the main enemy, the United States, dates back to Vladimir Lenin and Joseph Stalin. This projection process institutionalizes what can only be called political or nuclear paranoia in the realm of threat assessment and political analysis, as well as the personal predilections of Vladimir Putin and many other figures.[15] As this writer has observed elsewhere, Russian elites still officially subscribe to a watered down version of a Leninist threat paradigm that links together supposed internal "enemies" of the regime with outside powers, and this paradigm is regularly invoked by Russian authorities whenever problems manifest themselves.[16]

Indeed, it is not too much to say that there is a deeply held elite obsession with the United States as an exemplar enemy and potential partner, yet which is simultaneously regarded as being an *a priori* hostile power. This obsession with status, sovereignty, etc., and the U.S. attitude towards Russia, which is often perceived to be the mainspring of the overall U.S. international policy, contrasts sharply with the growing relative indifference in U.S. elite circles and U.S. society at large to Russia and its affairs.[17] Thus Richard Perle, former Assistant Secretary of Defense in the Ronald Reagan administration wrote about the U.S.-Russian relationship that:

> In fact, that relationship has declined in importance to the point where it makes little difference whether the Russians have more nuclear weapons or fewer than they do now. The calculations of the consequences of a nuclear exchange between the United States and Russia, a proper obsession during the Cold War, are no longer relevant, and despite President Obama's overblown claims, the New START Treaty is of no substantial benefit.[18]

This argument infuriates Russian elites, but there actually is considerable truth to it, as anyone observing the level of U.S. interest in Russia would quickly find out.

Another way of articulating this problem is to note that it is the fundamental nature of the Russian domestic political system, and a fact heightened by its juxtaposition to the U.S. and European systems, that drives the dynamic of hostility in East-West relations and fosters a situation where Russian thinking about security takes its cognitive and policy points of departure from what the German philosopher Carl Schmitt called the presupposition of conflict.[19] On a regular basis, the glaring asymmetries in the two sides' domestic political systems engender long-lasting perceptions based on mutual or reciprocal suspicion among powerful domestic constituencies that then try to obstruct meaningful progress in arms control or in overcoming outstanding differences on regional security issues in Eurasia. Consequently, any effort to determine not just Russia's posture but its evolving perspectives must take into account both the competing security orientations of the two states and the so-called values gap that fuels the mistrust, in order to understand Russian thinking to determine where accords can be reached or differences bridged and where they cannot be so resolved.

Meanwhile despite the treaty and the supposed bonhomie generated by the bilateral rapprochement, in 2010-11 the supposed U.S./NATO threat still drives Russian planning. We see this in many different expressions of Russian policy. For example, Dmitri Trenin has written that:

> To demonstrate how seriously the Kremlin views that issue of U.S. missile defense capabilities, look at Russia's national security strategy, released in May (2009). The document calls a U.S. first-strike capability, which is attainable once the United States builds a seamless global missile defense system, the most serious external military threat to Russia. Short of an actual first strike, a shift in the strategic balance would allow the United States to blackmail Russia politically. This may be paranoia, but there are reasons for it. In a situation when the United States and Russia are not allies, or even strategic partners, nuclear deterrence has become the unique pillar of Moscow's strategic independence vis-à-vis Washington.[20]

Similarly Dmitri Suslov also argues that Moscow considers the United States a "potential enemy" and seeks to maintain nuclear parity with it by any means and a quantitative advantage in TNW to include Anglo-French nuclear forces, which it also regards as hostile. Indeed, he observes that Russia is now discussing developing new types of nuclear missiles to compensate for the creation of missile defense elements within the NATO framework in Bulgaria, Romania, the Eastern Mediterranean, and Poland.[21] In a similar vein, it is not unusual to find in the Russian press analyses purporting to argue that despite the visible denuclearization of the U.S. arsenal, Washington still has plans that it is developing for a preemptive nuclear strike against Russia.[22]

By the same token, we find exceptionally well-connected analysts like Sergei Karaganov, Director of the Council on Foreign and Defense Policy, claiming that those pursuing nuclear zero are either motivated to or are unwittingly preparing trouble for Russia. Thus he writes that:

> It is obvious that the philosophy of mutual confrontation has not been overcome and has even received an energetic fillip as a result of the disarmament talks [this was before the treaty-author], although we do not actually threaten each other. We no longer have the contradictions whose resolution might envisage war, and we have many common interests. The professional 'disarmers' who have become more lively as a result of the treaty's success are ready to draw us into new disarmament races which will open new "Pandora's boxes." The American coalition of antinuclear dreamers and cold cynics, who were seeking to convert the United States' nonuclear superiority into political influence through the reduction of its nuclear arms that were cheapening it, has failed to launch movement toward a "nuclear zero." In addition, it turns out that it will not be possible to maintain even this superiority because of budget deficits in America.[23]

We also see this threat assessment in the new effort to create a force to keep the United States at bay.

President Dmitry Medvedev has recently decreed the creation of a new joint aerospace defense strategy and force structure combining existing air forces, antiaircraft, and ballistic missile defense (BMD) units with Russia's early warning system and space control assets that is to be organized by the end of 2011.[24] The subsequent creation of this new aerospace defense force (Vozdushno-Kosmicheskaya Oborona or VKO) with 70,000 new officers can only reinforce that threat perception, since it is precisely a NATO/U.S. air-space attack that is the scenario most dreaded by Russian planners.

In fact, Russian military leaders openly state that in the context of the concurrent negotiations that led to the treaty and its aftermath and Russia's defense reform that began in 2008, the role of the Strategic Rocket Forces (SRF) will actually grow despite the reductions in numbers.[25] Moreover, beginning in 2009 the Russian military began to modernize its nuclear arsenal with new systems, prolong existing ones, develop its command control capabilities, etc. In that context, the chief claim of the new RS-12 and RS-24 (Yars) missile systems is that they have independently targeted warheads and can evade (or so it is claimed) any Western missile defense, an attribute that allegedly fulfills former President Putin's earlier promise of asymmetric measures against U.S. missile defenses.[26] Simultaneously Russia is pursuing an agreement with the Obama administration that would give it access to U.S. technology for interceptors designed to destroy enemy missiles on impact.[27]

Although critics of the administration's policy point to this effort that is consonant with the administration's efforts to loosen export controls, reset with Russia, and move towards nuclear zero as a perfect storm; it is equally, if not even more, illustrative of the schizophrenic Russian atittude that while the United States is its main enemy, it also is the purveyor of the most desired and needed Russian defense technologies. Therefore, a reset or detente-like policy with America is needed.[28] Even after the treaty was signed, prominent defense commentators like Mikhail Barabanov wrote that the role of nuclear deterrence in Russian relations with the United States will actually grow because:

> The U.S. will never view Russia as a friend even in principle, because existence of other powerful countries is in principle unacceptable to America as the world hegemon, as they limit Washington's claims for world supremacy by the very fact of their existence. There are two such countries now, namely Russia and China. Actually this very fact is the main reason for tensions in the U.S.' relations with Russia and China under any regimes.[29]

Other arguments along this line, e.g., a recent commentary by Retired General M. A. Gareyev, President of the Academy of Military Sciences, typically contend that geopolitical pressures from the United States and China will only grow, that future wars may not be confined to local or regional theaters, and that "regarding security, Russia has never been in such a crunch as in the early 21st century since, perhaps, 1612." This is a rather bizarre and even hysterical threat perception for a World War II veteran.[30] Nevertheless, such analyses are all too visible in Russian public commentary on defense and security issues.

Meanwhile, this fear of such a U.S. and allied aerospace attack has been a major, though hardly the only, cause of both a dramatic increase in defense spending with these systems being a priority after nuclear weapons, and the termination of Russia's defense reform of 2008-11. The Russian press frequently comments about the potential for U.S. aerospace attack both by existing weapons and new ones in design like the X-37B *Orbital* Aircraft.[31] Increasingly Russian military writers see the air and space attack from the United States and/or NATO as an integrated operation, as in Libya and Kosovo, and regard it as the primary operational threat to Russia.[32] Since Russian analysts and officials regard U.S. conventional precision-strike capabilities as being strategic ones in their impact, they are not only striving to build an integrated aerospace defense against them but to use the treaty process, both in 2009-10 and in the future, as a means of reducing the threat.[33]

Indeed, so great is the perception of threat (before Libya) that Russia, in complete contradiction to the earlier defense reform's stated goals of reducing a bloated army and officer corps, created this new aerospace defense with 70,000 new officers at double pay, even as it sharply raises procurement targets. A new justification for this rise in defense spending, though it was planned no later than 2010, is the NATO intervention or air operation in Libya that officials from Premier Putin on down now claim justifies this immense expansion of defense spending. Thus a report on a recent visit to the defense plant in Votkinsk observed that:

> Putin pointed out that the enormous sums being invested in the State Defence Order are being diverted from other areas. And these sacrifices have to be justified. The state-of-the-art technologies that will emerge in the OPK will subsequently cross over into civilian sectors. And the events surrounding Libya also leave

the premier in no doubt regarding the necessity for and timeliness of the reinforcement of Russia's defense might. All too readily do the United States and its allies decide to employ armed force against sovereign states, Putin stressed.[34]

This argument also suggests that the Libyan operation will exact substantial costs upon the new reset policy of the Obama administration and Russo-American relations. All this is happening even as Russia cannot stop the insurgency that is inflaming the entire North Caucasus, and as its economy as a whole stagnates. Nor does it want to even study counterinsurgency to deal with this threat or the equally serious potential one of insurgency in Central Asia, as its response to ethnic pogroms in Kyrgyzstan in 2010 illustrates.[35]

Clearly, Russia also sees nothing wrong with missile defenses that can presumably take out the U.S. nuclear capability despite years of argumentation against BMD. But this new branch of the armed forces also shows the expectation of what Russian military writers believe would be the decisive first strike by U.S. and Allied forces, namely a conventional aerospace and missile attack supported by space-based or space-traversing assets.[36] Therefore, this enduring mistrust and melange of asymmetric cognitive approaches between Washington and Moscow are not simply a matter of differing ideas about the future trajectory of arms control and nonproliferation discussions. Rather, they continue to reflect and to express a fundamental clash of values that does not preclude negotiated treaties on arms control — which, after all, date back to 1963 — but which seriously impedes the process of reaching such accords.

One major consequence of this presumption of hostility that impedes, though it does not prevent, the reaching of accords with Moscow is that deep-rooted belief of the Russian leadership that due to this presumption of hostility, Russia must remain wedded to a posture of mutual assured destruction, mutual deterrence, and an almost literal and crude argument in favor of the offense-defense reaction described in earlier generations of writing on these subjects. From Russia's standpoint, the only way it can have security vis-à-vis the United States given that presupposition of conflict is if America is shackled to a continuation of the mutual hostage relationship based on mutual deterrence that characterized the Cold War, so that it cannot act unilaterally. To the degree that both sides are shackled to this mutual hostage relationship, Russia gains a measure of restraint or even of control over U.S. policy. For as Patrick Morgan has observed, this kind of classic deterrence "cuts through the complexities of needing to have a full understanding of or dialogue with the other side. Instead it enables a state, in this case Russia, to "simplify by *dictating*, the opponent's preferences."[37] (Italics in the original.) Thanks to such a mutual hostage relationship, Russian leaders see all other states who wish to attack them or even to exploit internal crises like Chechnya as being deterred. Therefore, nuclear weapons remain a critical component in the ensuring of strategic stability and, as less openly stated, in giving Russia room to act freely in world affairs.[38]

Russian Chief of Staff General Nikolai Makarov warned that:

The factor of parity should be accompanied by the factor of stability, if the U.S. missile defense begins to

14

evolve; it will be aimed primarily at destroying our nuclear missile capabilities. And then the balance of force will be tipped in favor of the United States.... With the existing and maintained parity of strategic offensive means, the global missile defense being created by the U.S. will be able to have some impact on the deterrence capabilities of the Russian strategic nuclear force already in the medium term....This may upset the strategic balance of force and lower the threshold for the use of nuclear weapons. Although missile defense is a defensive system, its development will basically boost [the] arms race.[39]

Neither is this just rhetoric. A recent article also points out that current Russian nuclear programs aim to overcome or even neutralize U.S. missile defenses.

The impression is that the Kremlin no longer believes in America's military omnipotence. Russia responded to the ultimatum with a maiden flight of its latest T-50 fighter and rearmament of its antiaircraft defense system with T-400 Triumph complexes. (This may be referring to what we call the S-400 SAM-author). To all appearances, Triumphs are ASAT weapons also capable of intercepting and destroying inbound ballistic warheads. Continuation of Bulava missile tests was proclaimed as well. Work on the missile will be brought to its logical end, sooner or later. Specialists are even working on a concept of the future strategic bombers that will replace TU-95s and Tu-160s one fine day.[40]

Since Moscow rigorously adheres to this mutual hostage concept, it cannot trust the United States, and any unilateral U.S. advance in defenses must be compensated by greater Russian offensive and defensive capabilities. For example, as noted above, missile defenses should lead Russia to procure missiles that can evade any defense. The following citations demonstrate this deep-rooted belief in the mutual hostage relationship, deterrence of the enemy, and the action-reaction process regarding armaments among the Russian political and military leadership. First, Lavrov told an interviewer in February 2007 that:

> Our main criterion is ensuring the Russian Federation's security and maintaining strategic stability as much as possible. . . . We have started such consultations already. I am convinced that we need a substantive discussion on how those lethal weapons could be curbed on the basis of mutual trust and balance of forces and interests. We will insist particularly on this approach. We do not need just the talk that we are no longer enemies and therefore we should not have restrictions for each other. This is not the right approach. It is fraught with an arms race, in fact, because, it is very unlikely that either of us will be ready to lag behind a lot.[41]

Here Lavrov signaled Russia's unwillingness to leave a mutually adversarial relationship with America and its presupposition of mutual hostility as reflected in both sides' nuclear deployments. Similarly, Alexei Arbatov then ridiculed the George H. Bush administration's view, stated by Ambassador Linton Brooks, the former U.S. arms control negotiator, that because the two sides are no longer adversaries, detailed arms control talks are no longer necessary, as either naiveté or outright hypocrisy.[42]

Since then Deputy Foreign Minister Sergei Ryabkov has stated that:

> Issues of strategic offensive and defensive arms are inextricably linked. To deny this relationship is meaningless because it is the essence of relations between

the countries that have the appropriate potential in both areas. An augmented capacity of one of the parties in the realm of missile defense is automatically echoed in the form of plans and decisions of the other party in the realm of strategic offensive arms. And not even obliquely, but in the most direct way what is happening in the field of missile defense and U.S. relations with its East European allies on this topic has an impact on our START follow-on negotiations. Without recognition of the relationship between strategic and offensive defensive arms, there can be no such treaty, it cannot take place.[43]

Likewise, Deputy Prime Minister Sergei Ivanov told the Munich Security conference in February 2010:

It is impossible to speak of reducing nuclear potentials in earnest while a state that possesses nuclear weapons is developing and deploying systems of defense against means of delivery of nuclear warheads that other states possess. It is like the sword and shield theory, where both are continuously developing with the characteristics and resources of each of them being kept in mind.[44]

Putin's late 2009 remarks in Vladivostok fit right into this outlook.

The problem is that our American partners are developing missile defenses, and we are not, . . . But the issues of missile defense and offensive weapons are closely interconnected. . . . There could be a danger that having created an umbrella against offensive strike systems, our partners may come to feel completely safe. After the balance is broken, they will do whatever they want and grow more aggressive.[45]

And this outlook has continued since the treaty was signed. As part of its ratification process, the Duma formally stated that both parties to the treaty accept that strategic offensive wapons and defenses are interrelated and that this relationship becomes more important as reductions in offensive systems occurs.[46] Similarly, Ivanov, speaking at the 2011 Munich Security conference stated that the creation of missile defenses leads to the development of strategic offensive weapon and thus a new arms race. Any efforts to buld a shield inevitably lead to comparable efforts to build a sword.[47]

REGIONAL SECURITY IN EURASIA IN RUSSIAN THINKING

Under the circumstances, it is not surprising that many Russian writers rightly attribute the persistence of deep mistrust despite our being 20 years past the end of the Cold War to the frozen mentality of deterrence and/or the mentality of a containment policy.[48] Thanks to all these factors that go into Russian thinking about arms control and nuclear weapons, the linkages between competing regional security policies and programs in Eurasia, and the two states' orientations to those issues, are invariably linked with with the agenda of arms control and nonproliferation negotiations, to cite some obvious examples. The current discussions on connecting Russia to the U.S. and NATO missile defense programs or the linkage between progress on the Conventional Armed Forces in Europe (CFE) treaty negotiations and the issue of TNW—including all of Russia—testifies to the abiding, if not growing, importance of these regional and strategic linkages.

In particular, for the Russian Federation this linkage between regional security and strategic agendas has become a paramount feature of overall Russian thinking about Russian security in both Europe and Asia. As Jacob Kipp has written:

> For Russia, which inherited the Soviet nuclear arsenal, but has faced a serious change in its international position, the nuclear equation is, in fact, shaped by Russia's status as a regional power in a complex Eurasian security environment, where nuclear issues are not defined exclusively by the U.S.-Russian strategic nuclear equation but by security dynamics involving interactions with Russia's immediate periphery. On the one hand, Russia's security responses have been shaped by a post-Soviet decade of sharp internal political crises, economic transformation, social instability, demographic decline, and the collapse of conventional military power. The impact of these developments has been uneven across Russia, leading to very distinct security environments which have demanded regional responses. The initial focus of security concerns for both the Soviet Union and the Russian Federation was primarily upon European security. This was the primary focus of the U.S.-Soviet strategic competition and the place where its militarization was most evident.[49]

Consequently, despite the treaty and the evident satisfaction of both parties with the current course of policy, the problems stemming from this fundamental disparity between them have not been overcome, and the reset policy is therefore subject to reversal, particularly if issues of regional security in Eurasia lead one or both sides to revert back to the presupposition of a conflicted relationship. If we are to understand the cognitive mainsprings of Russian thinking and security policy, we must further clarify this point of the nexus between regional and global security in Russian thinking and policy.

Fedor Lukyanov, like many others, has observed that while Russia has lost its global perspective, it seeks to retrieve it.[50] Andrei Tsygankov further amplifies this observation by stating that although Russia seeks to remain a regional power in Europe, the Caucasus, and Central and East Asia, it acts globally. In other words, it uses its geographical location astride several key Eurasian regions to force itself into both regional balances and thus leverage itself into being accepted as a global actor. To the extent that it feels itself excluded, as it did by the United States, from participating in key regional security fora, policies, or institutions, it pursues a policy of resistance using, among other instruments of power, its nuclear weapons.[51] As a result, and following Kipp's remarks above, from Russia's standpoint there can be no purely regional crisis in the key regions where it is situated or where it deems itself to have important interests. Consequently, the potential for any crisis to escalate, even against its participants' intentions, creates the ever-present possibility of a global crisis, if not conflict, where nuclear arms provide either the background music or are the primary instrumental soloists.[52]

This inherent linkage from the regional to the global level also shapes Russian approaches to the future agenda of arms control. Apart from the perceived linkages from regional to strategic level issues in Moscow's perspective, several prospective issues for future negotiations are intrinsically linked in Russian eyes. For example, the United States (and NATO) have long since argued that the next round of arms control treaty negotiations deal with the issues of TNW in Europe. Moscow has equally consistently rejected that stance, saying that countries owning or possessing TNW must first remove them to their home territory before any such talks could begin, thereby leaving Europe denuded of them. But now, according to Deputy Prime Minister Sergei Ivanov, Russia argues that, although it has repeatedly called on other nuclear states to remove TNW from abroad and leave them at home, restrict maneuvers with them on the territory of non-nuclear states, and disassemble structures for their prompt deployment abroad, "nonstrategic nuclear weapons grow increasingly outside NATO and Russia." In his words North Korea, Pakistan, Israel, and China are Russia's neighbors and their TNW, particularly China's, provide a threat.[53] While Ivanov's remarks should enlighten us concerning what Russia regards as its real strategic borders, what also is noteworthy that here is the announcement again, even if implicitly, that China and Israel are potential enemies and Pakistan is both a potential enemy and a proliferation threat.

Beyond the fact that this statement reflects a comparable presupposition of conflict with regard to all these states from Moscow's standpoint, Ivanov's remarks also reflect Moscow's posture that in any future round of arms control talks all nuclear states, not least China, should be at the table.[54] Makarov too has advocated bringing all nuclear powers to the table in the next negotiating round.[55] The Foreign Ministry has followed suit, saying the five major nuclear powers must join the next round of arms reductions talks.[56] Thus progress on TNW must somehow take account of the growing threat Russia perceives from China's increasing TNW threat, as well as its steadily developing conventional missiles and forces.[57] Other analogous linkages may well exist with regard to Russian perspectives on arms control issues. Again, for example, as Sam Nunn has argued, if there is to be success on curbing proliferation of nuclear (and chemical and biological) weapons, multilateral cooperation is essential. Thus other nuclear states must be fully committed partners.[58] Therefore, virtually every conceivable issue will play into the agenda of any future multilateral arms control negotiation, allowing any of those states to obstruct nonproliferation measures to secure its nuclear agenda, making cooperation on nonproliferation even more complicated than it has been in the past.

Ivanov's remarks fall into a broader context, namely that of the developing or growing Russian anxiety about Chinese military power and Russia's lack of anything near an adequate conventional response to it. There are multiplying signs of this anxiety and of Russia's efforts to reposture its conventional forces to deal with it. But of course, ultimately the TNW and other nuclear systems are the great equalizer in this theater, i.e., the Russian Far East (RFE).[59] By the time Moscow published its new defense doctrine in 2010, it had begun to consider the rise of China, not only as an example that could be emulated but also as a potential threat to the RFE. Thus the doctrine not only reiterated the by now long-standing invocation of a NATO threat, it also added new threats that appear to be focused, albeit without saying so, on China. Specifically, the 2010 doctrine cites a "show of military force with provocative objectives in the course of exercises on the territories of states contiguous with the Russian Federation or its allies" and "stepping up the activities of the armed forces of individual states (groups of states) involving partial or complete mobilization and the transitioning of these states' organs and military command and control to wartime operating conditions."[60]

Commentators here and abroad interpreted this language as pointing to the Russian perception of an increased potential Chinese threat based on the modernization of the Chinese armed forces and on exercises in 2009 that seemed to presage a possible mission directed against the RFE.[61] Indeed, in 2009 commanders for the first time began to speak publicly, undoubtedly with Moscow's assent, about a genuine military threat from China.[62] So while one motive for the Vostok-2003, and possibly the more recent Vostok -2010, exercise may be connected with the need to defend energy deposits in the RFE, a second motive clearly had to do with the rise of China.[63]

Vostok-2010 ended with a simulated tactical nuclear weapon strike on China to repel a ground invasion of Russia. Meanwhile, the extensive American coverage of China's new stealth Fighter, the J-20 and its naval construction program, including advanced anti-ship ballistic missiles (ASBMs), overlooks the fact that all these capabilities could be used against Russia as well. China has its own TNW, as well as thousands of conventional and nuclear missiles that could easily be targeted on Russia. As Kipp observed in 2010:[64]

A year ago, informed Russian defense journalists still spoke of the PLA [People's Liberation Army] as a mass industrial army seeking niche advanced conventional capabilities. Looking at the threat environment that was assumed to exist under Zapad 2009, the defense journalist Dmitri Litovkin spoke of Russian forces confronting three distinct types of military threats: "an opponent armed to NATO standards in the Georgian-Russian confrontation over South Ossetia last year. In the eastern strategic direction Russian forces would likely face a multi-million-man army with a traditional approach to the conduct of combat: linear deployments with large concentrations of manpower and firepower on different axis. In the southern strategic direction Russian forces expect to confront irregular forces and sabotage groups fighting a partisan war against 'the organs of Federal authority,' i.e., Internal troops, the border patrol, and the FSB [Federal Security Service]."[65] By spring of this year, a number of those involved in bringing about the "new look" were speaking of a PLA that was moving rapidly towards a high-tech conventional force with its own understanding of network-centric warfare.[66] Moreover, the People's Liberation Army conducted a major exercise "Stride-2009" which looked like a rehearsal for military intervention against Central Asia and/or Russia to some Russian observers.[67]

Beginning in 2009, overt discussions of the potential Chinese military threat began to surface in the military press. These statements were deliberately planned to call attention to Chinese military prowess.[68] And they all pointed to the threat of an invasion, not just by a large, multi-million man army, but also, as Roger McDermott observes, to the example derived from China's military modernization that has led China to an informatizing, if not informatized, high-tech capable military in just over a decade.[69] In a dilapidated and remote theater that is an economy of force theater with vast distances, inadequate infrastructure, and a declining industrial and manpower base:

> In the first instance, in any military conflict the Russian VVS (Air Forces) cannot guarantee air superiority against the Chinese. Moreover, they do not possess sensor-fused cluster munitions, though in theory their surface-to-surface missiles (SSM's) could deliver cluster munitions depending on whether the missile troops remained intact long enough. Faced with an advancing PLA division or divisions' early use of TNW would present a viable option.[70]

In this context, what is particularly telling about Russia and China's relations regarding the Arctic and Pacific energy deposits is the new trend in Russian naval policy; Russia's new plans for naval construction, especially in the RFE, also have access to the Arctic in mind.[71] Indeed, experts see the primary direction or mission of four new directions for the fleet and its new modernization program as being the protection of Russia's access to oil, gas, and other mineral reserves or deposits on Russia's continental shelf. All in all, 36 submarines and 40 surface ships are to be added by 2020.[72] But beyond this primary mission and the other three directions for future naval construction, these plans betray a reorientation of Russia's naval emphasis to the Asia-Pacific and to a new emphasis on meeting the challenge posed by China's naval buildup.[73] This naval construction is supposed to help Russia compensate for its vast conventional inferiority in numbers and quality vis-à-vis China in the RFE.[74]

Here we should understand that Russia's forces, particularly those in the North and the Far East may be deployed on a "swing basis" where either the Fleet or air forces in one theater move to support the fleet or air forces in the other. Russia has carried out exercises whereby one fleet moves to the aid of the other under such a concept.[75] Likewise, Russia has rehearsed scenarios for airlifting ground forces from the North to the Pacific in order to overcome the "tyranny of distance" that makes it very difficult for Russia to sustain forces in Northeast Asia. And the revival of regular air patrols over the oceans have clearly involved the Pacific-based units of the long range aviation forces as well as some of the air forces based in the north and Arctic that fly in the areas around Alaska.[76] Indeed, nuclear exercises moving forces or targeting weapons from the north to the Pacific or vice versa have also occurred.[77] To the degree that Arctic missions become part of the regular repertoire of the Russian armed forces, they will also to some degree spill over into the North Pacific. This all preceded Vostok-2010. Since then, China's military program has continued apace. Consequently, new Chinese developments like the conventional Intermediate Range Ballistic Missile (IRBM) DF-16, the new ASBM, etc. threaten not just the United States and its allies but also a whole range of Russian military targets deep into Russia.[78]

RUSSIA'S FORCE MODERNIZATION AND POSITIONS ON THE NEW NUCLEAR AGENDA

The foregoing perspectives are essential to understanding of Russian thinking as we discuss possibilities for future arms control negotiations involving Russia. In February-March 2011, Russian spokesmen outlined Russia's positions on almost all the outstanding issues for a future arms control negotiation. Russia's positions concerning the evolving nuclear agenda as well as its ongoing weapons program reflect its assessment not only of the situation created by the new treaty but also its assessment of current or future threats and longstanding Russian policy objectives.

First of all, Russia is currently undertaking its newest in a series of long-term defense modernization projects. The State Armament Program submitted to Medvedev and the Duma for 2011-20 now totals 20.7 trillion rubles ($646 billion), of which 19.4 trillion rubles goes to the needs of the Ministry of Defense. Of that total, 79 percent will go to the acquisition and purchase of high-tech armaments (including nuclear weapons, which remain a priority). This represents a tripling of the current 2006-15 program that supposedly provides for delivery of 1,300 models of equipment and armament, of which 220 require modernization or creation of new capacities.[79] Within this new program, which also entails the comprehensive modernization of the entire machine tool sector along with the high-tech sector, the state order (Goszakaz) for 2011 will go up by a third to 1.5 trillion rubles in 2011 and then another third by 2013 to 2 trillion rubles.[80] Right now, there is a serious debate regarding the nuclear sector. Many defense industry sectors possess the ambition to virtually double ICBM (intercontinental ballistic missile) production through 2020 by modernizing production lines and producing heavy liquid-propellant missiles and are spending nearly 77 billion rubles towards these ends.[81] Russia aims to modernize its quantitative arsenal to conform to the new treaty's requirements. Furthermore, because it maintains that the United States has not definitively settled upon a missile defense model (which is strange given the administration's policy), it allegedly needs to modernize qualitatively to have designs that can counter space weapons, a set of weapons that Moscow apparently fully believes the United States intends to create.[82]

Therefore, one way to meet these demands is to create a heavy liquid-propelled ballistic missile, an issue that has touched off a major debate among missile designers with First Deputy Defense Minister Vladimir Popovkin supporting it, and Yuri Solomonov, a famous missile designer at the Moscow Institute of Thermal Technology, opposing it. In opposition to the calls for this new missile are the designers of the Topol-M, Yars, and Bulava solid propellant systems. In other words, Russia's nuclear program, although work has started on the liquid-propellant system, is in the throes of a debate, so its final outcome and prognosis remain somewhat unclear at this time.[83] Despite this as yet unresolved debate, the current expectation is that the ultimate design will copy that of the Satan (SS-18) ICBM and be insensitive to the effect of an electromagnetic (EMP) impulse, launchable from a silo even after a missile has hit it, and capable of carrying a large complex of defense penetration aids so that it can evade missile defenses and deliver a 10-ton combat payload to any point in the world. It also will include 10 individually-guided warheads of the megaton class, i.e., it will be a multiple independently targetable reentry vehicle (MIRV).[84] These plans date back at least to 2008 when it was first announced that the new RS-24 would be MIRVed.[85]

Meanwhile Deputy Defense minister Vladimir Popovkin is moving forward and outlining a huge Russian conventional and nuclear rearmament program through 2020.

Popovkin said Russia plans to develop a new liquid-fueled heavy ICBM to carry up to ten warheads, and having a service life of up to 35 years. Former RVSN [Russian Strategic Missile Forces] Commander General-Lieutenant Andrey Shvaychenko talked about a new liquid heavy missile as far back as late 2009, and the issue's been debated in the Russian military press since. Popovkin said the Defense Ministry plans to accept the Bulava SLBM [submarine-launched ballistic missle] and the first two *Borey*-class SSBNs [ship, submersible, ballistic, nuclear] this year. There will be 4-5 Bulava launches this year. Recall [that] to date only 7 of 14 Bulava tests have been successful. Addressing the missile's past failures, Popovkin said there were many deviations from the design documentation during production. He also said Russia plans to build eight SSBNs to carry Bulava by 2020. He was unclear if this includes the first two *Borey*-class boats.[86]

It is clear that this construction program contemplates, not just deterrence, but a war using nuclear weapons, albeit in what is possibly a restricted number of contingencies but clearly premised on a U.S./NATO attack. Indeed, as Popovkin said in another interview, the first priority is the strategic deterrent, which includes nuclear weapons, early warning, and missile and aerospace defense (i.e., the new VKO force).

> The first priority [is] the strategic deterrent force. They have two components: the strategic nuclear forces, as well as a system of missile warning, missile defense and aerospace defense. The second priority [is] a long list of high-precision weapons, whose use is based on information support from space. Third - automated command and control systems [ACCS]. In the next 2 or 3 years, [it is proposed] to link all species of ACCS in a single management system. Modernize it so it was with an open architecture and it allows you to build the capacity in any direction.[87]

Finally, as part of the nuclear program the General Staff commissioned research institutes to determine how many nuclear warheads are needed for a guaranteed retaliatory strike against a potential enemy, presumably to confirm the General Staff's earlier insistence on 1,500 warheads as an irreducible minimum under present circumstances.[88] These studies and building programs obviously have a great deal of bureaucratic muscle and financing behind them, so in practical terms it will be very difficult to win Russian assent to large reductions in strategic forces until and unless other nuclear powers, including but in addition to the United States, also agree to them. This makes attaining the goal of nuclear zero anytime soon a very dubious proposition.

However, beyond this set of considerations, there are also other reasons for suspecting that, despite the effort to complete a huge conventional upgrading of the Russian military, Russia in 2015-20 will continue relying much more on nuclear weapons and nuclear deterrence. Basically, it has already become clear that defense industry, which has never been able to provide the armed forces with its requirements, has again failed as of 2010. Recent articles make the extent of this failure very clear. Specifically:

> Last year, for example, they did not get a single nuclear submarine cruiser, although the *Yuri Dolgoruky* with 12 Bulava missiles on board and a multirole *Yasen*-class nuclear submarine were to have been commissioned at the very least, and only 5 out of 11 communications and reconnaissance satellites were sent into space. Nor did the fleet get a project 20380 *corvette*. Only six out of nine *Yak*-130 aircraft planned for delivery were received and just 78 out of 151 BMP-3 infantry fighting vehicles.[89]

Yet, typically, nobody received a public reprimand for this confirming that "nonfulfillment of the Army's orders in the defense industry has become the norm for our country."[90] Under the circumstances, the planned modernization of the forces' armaments remains an equally dubious proposition. But, in turn, that raises the question of how the military is to fulfill President Medvedev's 2008 directive that by 2020 Russia should have:

> A guaranteed nuclear deterrent system for various military and political circumstances must be provided by 2020. . . . We must ensure air superiority, precision strikes on land and sea targets, and the timely deployment of troops. We are planning to launch large-scale

production of warships, primarily, nuclear submarines with cruise missiles and multi-purpose attack
submarines. . . . We will also build an air and space
defense network.[91]

Furthermore, the planned conventional modernization also seemed to imply an interest in exploring
the possibilities for more sophisticated conventional
means of deterrence. Thus former Deputy Defense
Minister and current Duma member Andrei Kokoshin
called the *Severodvinsk* class of fourth generation nuclear powered but conventionally armed submarines a
non-nuclear deterrent, suggesting this interest in non-
nuclear forms of deterrence and of a concept of deterrence "ladders," some or most of which would only
require the use or display of conventional systems.[92]
Absent sufficient capabilities of this kind, Russia will
have little choice but to rely predominantly on nuclear
deterrence against the United States (NATO), China,
and potential proliferators in its vicinity. Yet as Medvedev and Defense Minister Serdyukov have publicly
said, Moscow will not even be able to reach the treaty's limits for nuclear weapons by 2020, forcing it both
to modernize its existing arsenal, i.e., MIRVs, extend
existing weapons past that date, and hope for the best
regarding conventional systems until 2020.[93] Therefore, the already visible failure of Russia's modernization project adds another to a long series of question
marks that must be put against the idea of obtaining
serious nuclear reductions in the foreseeable future.
Indeed, Kokoshin has said that nuclear deterrence
will remain the keystone of Russian defense for the future, that there are no conceivable alternatives to nuclear deterrence even in the distant future (i.e., the presupposition of hostility with both the West and China,

not to mention everyone else cited here, will continue till then). Therefore Russia must continue modernizing its land, sea, and air-based nuclear weapons and its tactical and operational-tactical nuclear systems, too.[94]

RUSSIAN PERCEPTIONS OF THE NEW TREATY

Russian perceptions of where it stands as a result of the new treaty also represent an obstacle to progress because they are firmly ensconced in the matrix of the mutual hostage and presumption of hostility mentioned above. Deputy Defense Minister Anatoly Antonov, who negotiated the treaty, calls it the gold standard for future treaty negotiations.[95] He and his colleagues certainly regard it favorably but largely because it reduced the U.S. threat and strengthened Russia's relative position, not that it enhanced international security. Lavrov echoed Antonov's description of the treaty.[96] Serdyukov stated that not only does the treaty provide a guaranteed level of deterrence adequate to Russia's security; it allows Russia to update 70 percent of strategic carriers and warheads or 90 percent of those belonging to the Strategic Missile Troops, while America must reduce its arsenal. Like Lavrov, he said that if the United States continues to build missile defenses, the treaty allows Russia to make "an adequate response, i.e., withdraw from the treaty."[97] Medvedev's national security advisor, Sergei Prikhodko, voiced his approval of the clauses limiting deployed delivery vehicles and launch systems and the incorporation of heavy bombers into those categories that limit U.S. breakout potential, a key Russian demand.[98]

Other commentators cheered the reduction of inspection visits to each other's facilities, which they regarded as burdensome and as a means of transmitting intelligence data to Washington. Therefore, they also cheered the elimination of the requirement for transmitting remote telemetry of test launches of news missiles for the same reasons. Russia also secured exemption for monitoring for road-mobile Topol land-based ICBMs. Getting the United States to count some conventional carriers as strategic ones, equating them to nuclear weapons in line with Russian assessments of those systems, is another positive outcome from Russia's point of view. Yet Russia's capabilities for building up its arsenal were not affected. At the same time, of course, the treaty was a compromise and reflected some American gains, namely, safeguarding the missile defense program and on verification.[99] Similarly, Ruslan Pukhov, a noted defense commentator, observes that these benefits for Russia, along with the overall reduction of both sides' nuclear potential, is very beneficial for Russia and that, "It is obvious that this is not very beneficial for the U.S. on the whole."[100] Likewise, Alexei Arbatov argues that the treaty limits both U.S. nuclear and conventional strategic forces and gives Russia means of leverage upon the United States.[101] For these reasons, given the Russian sense of having won or at least prevailed in the negotiations, it is hardly surprising that Antonov said further disarmament is contingent upon both sides implementing the treaty (presumably with the hidden implication that should the United States build defenses, Russia might exercise its option for withdrawal).[102] Unfortunately, it is precisely these Russian gains that have aroused the ire of Republican opponents of the treaty in the United States and underscores the continuing bilateral mistrust that could yet poison the reset policy and future arms control talks, not to mention progress towards a nuclear zero.

Finally, in advance of a new round of negotiations, there is a decided difference in the contending approaches of Russia and the United States. As recently reported in connection with Deputy Foreign Minister Ryabkov's recent visit to the United States:

> While U.S. officials have focused publicly on a nuclear treaty that would cover reducing the numbers of not just strategic arms but also shorter-range tactical nuclear weapons, Ryabkov talked first about turning to the control of conventional arms in Europe and reaching some predictability of forces on the continent. He said shaping the military relationships on the ground, where Russia has vastly fewer troops and less equipment, would relate to the future of nuclear disarmament. He [Ryabkov] talked about the difficulty of finding the correct "platform" for any future agreements, saying that weapons in outer space, non-nuclear strategic weapons, other nuclear nations and missile defenses also have to be considered.[103]

This last impediment to future reductions and progress to nuclear zero is hardly insurmountable in and of itself. But added to the existing obstacles, and to the pressure of unforeseen events like Libya, all of these obstacles to further reductions represent serious obstructions to negotiations toward that end. For example, in earlier statements Ryabkov also heightened the importance of serious efforts to settle regional conflict that upset stability globally.[104]

PROLIFERATION

The two outstanding and unresolved issues of nuclear proliferation, Iran and North Korea, also pose significant challenges to any enduring Russo-American reset policy, let alone amity and genuine cooperation on international security. Indeed, the two governments' divergent approach to these issues reflects wide conceptual and perceptual gaps between them. It is safe to say that for almost 20 years, proliferation has become a virtual obsession of U.S. policymakers who, nonetheless, have little to show for this obsession. Indeed, we went to war in Iraq over this issue, only to entrap ourselves. We see proliferation as jeopardizing the global and regional nuclear order, threatening U.S. allies in the Middle East and East Asia, and deterring our ability to project conventional military power throughout the world. But we do not really focus on the regional security dynamics of these issues in the way that Moscow does. Instead, Russia views these issues primarily as regional security challenges or in that context where the linkages discussed above between regional security in key areas and Russian national security assume mounting importance. Given Russia's ambitions to challenge the United States regionally through the formation of counterbalances to it, the result is a set of contending issues where Russia sees us as threatening principles and interests that it deems central to its security.

Moscow firmly opposes adding new members to the nuclear club and regards proliferation as a threat. Therefore it has worked with Washington to eliminate "loose nukes" and to discourage new states in the Commonwealth of Independent States (CIS) or former Warsaw Pact members from expanding earlier nuclear programs. It has steadily (at least rhetorically) claimed that it is seeking to channel Iran's nuclear program into one supervised by the International Atomic Energy Agency (IAEA).[105] Russia has also established controls over foreign economic operations with nuclear materials, special non-nuclear materials and corresponding technologies, as well as dual-use goods and technology, principally as a component of the policy of nonproliferation. The Export Control Law, adopted in 1999, has locked in the term "Export Control" specifically for this sphere. The 1995 Law on national regulation of foreign trading activities described Export Control as the full set of measures for the implementation of a "transfer procedure" for agreed-upon goods, technologies, and services. The 1999 law codified this term as "foreign trading, investment, and other activities, including production cooperation in the field of the international exchange of goods, information, work, services, and results of intellectual activities, including exclusive rights to them (intellectual property)." This means not only the export of goods and technologies abroad, but also their transfer to a foreigner within the territory of the Russian Federation. In January 1998, the Russian government introduced rules for "all-encompassing control" (catch-all).[106]

Nonetheless, Moscow has repeatedly stated that on nonproliferation issues it follows its own interests. While Russia regards proliferation as a threat, it comes fifth in Russia's new defense doctrine after a whole series of U.S.-inspired threats like NATO enlargement and missile defenses. Moreover, the doctrine explicitly states that Russia expects that by 2020 it will be living in a proliferated world.[107] In early 2002, Defense Minister Sergei Ivanov outlined Russian thinking and policy concerning proliferation.

Russia scrupulously adheres to its international obligations in the sphere of non-proliferation of mass destruction weapons, means of their delivery, and corresponding technologies. The key criteria of Russian policy in this sphere are our own national security, the strengthening of our country's international positions and the preservation of its great power status.[108]

Therefore, Russia evaluates proliferation issues not according to whether the regime is democratic or not, but on the basis of whether a country's nuclearization would seriously threaten Russia and its interests.[109] In commenting on President Putin's June 2007 proposal to let the Americans jointly manage the Russian missile defense radar at Gabala, Azerbaijan, Chief of Staff General Yuri N. Baluyevsky stated that Washington's claim that Russia now admitted to an Iranian threat was a misinterpretation. While Russia never denied a global threat of nonproliferation of missiles and nonproliferation, "we insist that this trend is not something catastrophic, which would require a global missile defense system deployed near Russian borders."[110] More recently, Serdyukov stated that, "We don't share all the West's views on the capacities of the Iranian nuclear program."[111] Likewise, Lavrov and his Deputy Sergei Ryabkov state that though sanctions might become inevitable if Iran does not comply with the IAEA regarding enrichment of uranium; Iran represents no threat to Europe or America. Moreover, Moscow has no evidence of its planning a military nuclear program that would justify missile defenses.[112] Moscow's continuing opposition to U.S. missile defenses partly stems from that outlook.

Accordingly, Moscow tends to view American policy towards nonproliferation in jaundiced fashion, displaying a visible *Schadenfreude* when North Korea tested missiles and then a nuclear weapon in July and October 2006.[113] Or Russian officialdom often views Washington's insistence on nonproliferation controls as mainly an effort to pressure competitors in the nuclear and arms markets.[114] Russia's new defense doctrine openly says that the number of states having nuclear weapons will increase.[115] While this might be regarded as a negative trend, it is certainly strange to concede proliferation in advance of the fact. At the same time, Russian leaders also publicly say that this is mainly a U.S., not necessarily a Russian, concern.

Alexei Arbatov's 2009 analysis of Russian thinking about proliferation represents the most detailed explication of Russia's approach. As Arbatov notes:

> For Russia the acquisition of nuclear weapons and ballistic missiles by India and Pakistan and the prospects of further proliferation are adding some new elements to a familiar and old threat, rather than creating a dramatic new one, as is the case with the United States. The USSR and Russia have learned to live with this threat and to deal with it on the basis of nuclear deterrence, some limited defenses (like the Moscow BMD system and national Air Defenses) and through diplomacy, which is used to avoid direct confrontation (and still better, to sustain normal relations) with new nuclear nations.[116]

Other analysts confirm that Russia responded to Indo-Pakistani proliferation in a low-key manner and that Russian elites still regard America as the only or most likely potential adversary.[117] Instead, Moscow regards vertical proliferation (qualitative improvement) as opposed to horizontal proliferation of nuclear weapons to new states with greater alarm than does the United States. Russia's posture thus reverses America's that takes greater alarm at horizontal proliferation.[118]

So while nuclear and missile proliferation are serious Russian security issues, not least because of Russia's geographical proximity to all existing and potential proliferators, Russia does not profess undue alarm at this trend. Unlike America, it advances no claim to be a global "policeman," does not deploy military sites or armed forces abroad (except in some post-Soviet states) and does not employ its forces in serious combat operations. In fact, Russia's greatly reduced conventional power capabilities, coupled with its expansive geopolitical ambitions, are leading it to become a major exporter of sensitive nuclear technologies to would be proliferators as it seeks to reduce U.S. influence in world politics.[119] Thus it avoids challenging other countries, including actual or potential nuclear and missile-capable regimes. Due to Russia's vulnerability and lack of reliable security protection and commitments from other nations, its nonproliferation stance is much more cautious and flexible than that of the United States. Indeed, it sees the Democratic People's Republic of Korea (DPRK) and Iran as potential partners, not enemies, and therefore will not categorically oppose their programs, as does Washington.

Moreover, given Russia's post Cold War weakness, it has been forced to confront other security threats that are incomparably more urgent to it than proliferation. These threats, as listed by Arbatov, comprise:

- The instability and bloody conflicts across the post-Soviet space and in the North Caucasus of Russia proper (which has a 1,000 kilometer (km) common border with the volatile South Caucasus).

- NATO's continuous extension to the east against strong Russian objections.
- Continuing stagnation of Russian armed forces and defense industries and Russia's growing conventional and nuclear inferiority to the United States and NATO.
- The threat of expanding Muslim radicalism in the Central Asia (7,000 km of common border with Russia).
- The scary growth of economic and military power of China (5,000 km of common border with Russia).
- The United States plans to deploy missile defenses in Eastern Europe.[120]

Arbatov further observes that:

> There is a broad consensus in Russia's political elite and strategic community that there is no reason for their nation to take U.S. concerns closer to heart than its own worries - in particular if Washington is showing neither understanding of those problems of Russia, nor any serious attempts to remove or alleviate them in response for closer cooperation with Russian on non-proliferation subjects. [121]

Finally, Iran is an extremely important geopolitical partner of Russia's, a growing "regional superpower" that balances out the expansion of Turkey and the increasing U.S. military and political presence in the Black Sea/Caspian region and Middle East, and simultaneously contains Sunni Wahhabism's incursions in the North Caucasus and Central Asia.[122] Russia also views Iran as the dominant regional power in the neighborhood who can project power into the Caucasus, Central Asia, and the Persian Gulf. Therefore,

Moscow values Iran's refraining from doing just that by its pro-Iranian policies.[123] Likewise, Russia does not take the proliferation threat nearly as seriously as does the United States and its allies in Europe and the Middle East.[124] Consequently it views the current situation in Iran and North Korea quite differently than does the United States.

Iran.

For the United States, Iran is the primary test case of Russian support for nonproliferation, and the current administration, like its predecessor, has invested enormous time and effort in obtaining Russian support. The administration evidently believes that America needs Russian support to curb Iran's proliferation threat and obviously this dictates some concessions to Russia in return for its support of U.S. efforts. According to administration spokesmen like Michael McFaul of the National Security Council, if Russia wanted an adversarial relationship with the United States on Iran, there are many things that it could do to but has not done to worsen the U.S. situation there.[125] President Obama has voiced his optimism that the United States, with Russian (and Chinese) cooperation will secure "tough, strong sanctions" on Iran.[126]

Despite the reset policy's gains whereby Russia has refrained from selling Iran the S-300 and voted for United Nations Security Council (UNSC) Resolution 1964 imposing sanctions on Iran, this ongoing crisis underscores the divergent perspectives between Moscow and Washington. But it also demonstrates how Russia utilizes the Iranian issue as part of its approach to the United States. Thanks to the reset policy, the administration has at least for now substantially altered the correlations between U.S.-Russia and Russo-Iranian relations by demonstrating to Moscow that it can make gains with the United States in return for more distancing from Iran. Clearly, Russia's decision made in September 2010 to cancel the sale of the S-300 anti-air missile to Iran closely correlates with the improvement of Moscow's ties to Washington.[127] Thus in September 2010, Moscow invoked the United Nations (UN) sanctions resolution for which it voted as grounds for terminating the sale of the S-300 and even returning the money paid for it to Iran, despite the fact that it could have exempted such sales and stay within the language of the resolution.[128] Indeed, earlier Russian and Chinese pressure had led the United States to weaken its originally intended list of sanctions directed against Iran.[129] So, clearly, the administration's belief that it had an understanding with the Russian government was validated by the decision to terminate the sale of the S-300. As a result, the administration may well argue that its stance is justified by Russia's termination of the sale of the S-300 to Iran.[130]

As Arbatov also observes, unlike America, Russia does not view North Korea and Iran as potential enemies. Iran is a major consumer of Russian arms, which helps the military-industrial sector to survive, given many years of limited defense orders for the Russian armed forces. Finally, Iran is an extremely important geopolitical partner of Russia's, a growing "regional superpower" that balances out the expansion of Turkey and the increasing U.S. military and political presence in the Black Sea/Caspian region and Middle East, and simultaneously contains Sunni Wahhabism's incursions in the North Caucasus and Central Asia.[131] Russia also views Iran as the dominant regional power in the neighborhood who can project power into the Caucasus, Central Asia, and the Persian Gulf. Therefore, Moscow, by its pro-Iranian policies, values Iran's refraining from doing so.[132] Likewise, Russia does not take the proliferation threat nearly as seriously as does the United States and its allies in Europe and the Middle East.[133]

For example, diplomat Gleb Ivashentsov, then Director of the Second Asia Department in the Russian Foreign Ministry, told a Liechtenstein Colloquium on Iran in 2005 that:

> Iran today is probably the only country in the greater Middle East that, despite all of the internal and external difficulties, is steadily building up its economic, scientific, technological, and military capability. Should this trend continue, Iran—with its seventy million population, which is fairly literate, compared to neighboring states, and ideologically consolidated, on the basis of Islamic and nationalist values; with a highly intellectual elite, with more than eleven percent of the world's oil and eighteen percent of natural gas reserves; with more than 500,000 strong armed forces and with a strategic geographic position enabling it to control sea and land routes between Europe and Asia—is destined to emerge as a regional leader. This means that the Islamic Republic of Iran will be playing an increasing role in resolving problems not only in the Middle East and Persian Gulf area but also in such regions that are rather sensitive for Russia as Transcaucasia, Central Asia and the Caspian region. This is why dialogue with Iran and partnership with it on a bilateral and regional as well as a broad international basis is objectively becoming one of the key tasks of Russia's foreign policy.[134]

Similarly Matthew Kroenig has more recently written that:

> In fact, Russia and China have not been willing to authorize tough sanctions against Iran's nuclear program, not primarily because they have important economic interests in country as many analysts believe, but because they are not particularly threatened by Iran's nuclear development. Russia and China are not currently operating military forces in the Middle East and, given the degradation of Russia's military since the end of the Cold War and China's military modernization focusing on a Taiwan Straits contingency, it is very unlikely that these countries will have the capability to do so for the foreseeable future. For this reason, they do not need to worry that nuclear proliferation in Iran will constrain the military freedom of action. They might be concerned that Iran could attack them in the bolt-out-of-the-blue nuclear strike, or provide nuclear weapons to terrorists who might target them, but such scenarios are extremely unlikely. In sum, Beijing and Moscow have very little to fear from nuclear proliferation in Iran. They are unwilling to place serious pressure on Tehran and are willing to continue economic relations with the country, given that many strategic thinkers in Russia and China believe that what is bad for Washington must be good for Moscow and Beijing, some foreign officials undoubtedly welcome Iranian nuclear development as a means of tying down the United States. [135]

Yet Iran still defies the IAEA, enriches uranium, and builds new nuclear centers.[136] Nonetheless, in August 2010 Moscow completed the Bushehr reactor and opened it to production, lest it lose Iranian cooperation and the huge sums invested there. Bushehr's opening underscores the continuing unilateralism of Russia's Iran policy and the limited scope or cooperation with Washington on that issue.

Neither have Iran's sharp polemics on the S-300 nor Moscow's threat of sanctions should Iran fail to accept enrichment outside Iran and IAEA monitoring led to any sign that Moscow will support truly meaningful sanctions on Iran. Indeed, when after the June 2010 UNSC resolution, the United States and the European Union (EU) imposed their own further sanctions on Iran, Moscow called those new sanctions "unacceptable" and warned again that the use of force could lead to disaster.[137] In mid-July, Russian Energy Minister Sergei Shmatko and Iranian Oil Minister Masoud Mirkazemi jointly announced a 30-year road map for bilateral cooperation in oil and gas.[138] The large deals mapped out as part of that partnership include cooperation on the transportation, swaps, and marketing of natural gas; sales of petroleum products and petrochemicals, and Russia's establishment of a $100 million liquefied natural gas (LNG) plant to supply remote regions of Iran.[139] Shmatko made it clear that Russia would not accept sanctions other than those of the UNSC, that those sanctions did not apply to this new deal, and that Russia would not be hindered by the existing sanctions in drawing up energy cooperation plans with Iran. Indeed, he saw no limits to bilateral energy cooperation. Russia also apparently was involved in May in trying to broker an Irano-Turkish-Brazilian deal to swap low-enriched uranium fuel for higher enriched fuel for medical reactors.[140]

Despite warnings to Iran, Moscow still formally opposes "paralyzing sanctions," the only kinds that make sense. Medvedev speaks of "smart sanctions" and clarified to Washington the limits of what Russia will support to meet the twin objectives of inducing Iran to stop enrichment and weaponization; and second, to advance Russian interests.[141] Moreover, the smart sanctions that Moscow now advocates would not amount to an arms or energy embargo on Iran. Even now Lavrov and Ryabkov state that though sanctions might become inevitable if Iran does not comply with the IAEA regarding enrichment of uranium, Iran represents no threat to Europe or the United States. Moreover, Moscow has no evidence of Iran planning a military nuclear program that would justify missile defenses.[142] Similarly, Andranik Migranyan, Director of the Kremlin-backed Institue for Democracy and Cooperation in New York said that Russian cooperation with the United States on further sanctions against Iran is "highly unlikely." He further stated that for the United States to get Russian support Moscow would have to be "duly compensated," i.e., bribed, by ceasing NATO enlargement, missile defense deployments, the rearming of the Georgian Army, "blunt and unceremonious interference" in the internal affairs of the new republics, and any assistance to political forces who are hostile to Russia.[143] In other words, Russia will distance itself from Iran to the degree that Washington guarantees it undisputed hegemony in the CIS and Eurasia. Most recently, Russia now objects to the publication of a new UN report on Iran describing Iranian violations of UN sanctions resolutions against it.[144]

While Russia professes to oppose Iranian nuclearization (and supports the plan to bring Iranian nuclear spent fuel to Russia), it has been a prime supporter of the process, exporting scientists and technologists to Iran throughout the 1990s and providing major assistance for Iran's conventional weapon, space, and missile programs.[145] Some recent reports actually allege the existence of a long-term high-level Russian program to smuggle weapons clandestinely into Iran, using the Algerian and Syrian governments, Kurdish terrorists, and members of Russian organized crime in Spain.[146] Moreover, many Russians have persuaded themselves that Washington owes Moscow something in regard to Europe and the Middle East.[147]

Clearly, it seems that key sectors like the energy and arms sectors in Moscow are impeding any effort to cooperate with Washington. This bears out what we have said above. In particular, we see a time-honored Russian negotiating tactic. As Vladimir Socor writes:

> First, Moscow approved the sanctions resolution after almost two years of procrastination, watering it down and leaving the S-300 issue ambiguous. During this time the Obama Administration saw its leeway in Eurasia constrained by the quest for Russian support against Iran. In the next stage (now) implementation turns out to be subject to a Russian "mechanism" yet to be defined (to be negotiated). Classically Russia makes a deal cashing in a quid-pro-quo, only to start negotiating again for the deal's implementation subject to some other quid-pro-quo. In the third stage, it will be up to Russia's president to list the sanctions-banned weapons, and by the same token, to omit certain items, leaving Russia free to deliver these to Iran. Thus the Kremlin will ultimately interpret the UN Security Council resolution on the S-300's and not only on this issue.[148]

It is not difficult to decipher what quid-pro-quos Moscow now seeks. According to Fedor Lukyanov:

> There will be no automatic agreement by Russia to toughen the sanctions. In Moscow's opinion, it has already gone very far as it is; . . . But Russia's support of the sanctions in May and generally the marked change in position in the last six months are above all the result of the "exchange" of the Iranian question for no

deployment of missile defense in Eastern Europe. For Moscow to go further, a new understanding is needed, although at this point it is unclear on what. A great deal depends on the ratification of the START treaty; if its ratification in the US Senate fails, that will have an effect on all the related topics, including Iran.[149]

This is now an urgent question, as Iran claims to have obtained S-300 missiles and is moving ahead on its satellite and nuclear programs to the best of its ability.[150] Although Russia has denied selling or transferring these missiles, as has Ukraine; if these claims are true, the missiles could only have come from Russia and/or through the support of some third party like Belarus and Ukraine, which Russia has used in the past to sell abroad weapons with which it did not want to be publicly associated. Moreover, it is clear to any observer that Russia's arms sales program is riddled with massive corruption that could conceivably allow for such sales to occur.[151]

This outlook should not have eluded U.S. commentators for, as John Parker observes in his masterful study of Russo-Iranian relations:

> No matter how much Russia and the United States might share security concerns over Iran's nuclear program and expanding influence in the Middle East, a common approach by Washington and Moscow was always undercut by Russia's rivalry with the United States other interests in Iran, and the historical approach to dealing with that country.[152]

That historical approach, as Parker demonstrates, is one that recognized that Russia must always have close relations with Iran as a neighbor, even though it could ultimately represent a threat to Russia because of its missile and nuclear programs. Indeed, already in 1993, Moscow recognized that those programs could represent a threat to its territory, neighbors, and vital interests.[153] This is one reason why the Russian government has continued to sell Iran weapons after 1992: precisely because it recognized that Iran had the potential to disrupt the Caucasus, Central Asia, and even possibly Afghanistan, Moscow realized that it had to blend arms sales with close monitoring by its security service in regard to Iranian activities.[154] Economic calculations to keep defense industry markets and preserve that sector, in addition to Russia's long-standing and probably not unfounded belief that if it did not sell weapons to Iran, Europe and the United States would do so, also drive Moscow's large arms sales program to Iran. Therefore, arms sales to Iran have always been an arrow in Moscow's quiver to prevent Iran from pursuing a policy of interference in the border regions, and it has succeeded handsomely from Russia's point of view.[155] To openly renege on outstanding contracts, e.g., the S-300 surface to air missile, would not only cause financial losses and Iranian anger and distrust of Russian promises, it could also open the door to Iranian retaliation. Therefore, Russia has found it difficult to take Western concerns seriously.

Indeed, if we understood Russian policy correctly, we would not invest misplaced hopes in them. Russian commentary on the recent oil and gas and nuclear energy agreements indicates this. First, it appears that one reason why Russia finally finished the Bushehr project is because of its fears that Iran might conclude a deal with other providers of peaceful nuclear energy, e.g., Japan.[156] This determination not to allow others to replace Russia in Iranian calculations fully comports with 20 years of policy delineated by Parker. Second, Russian official and expert commentary on Bushehr reveals Moscow's stance on Iran quite clearly. Officials and experts say this collaboration represents a diplomatic victory for Russian diplomacy, carries no risks for Russia, shows Iran's right to peaceful nuclear energy, supposedly keeps Iran in the nonproliferation regime thereby saving the Nonproliferation Treaty (NPT) even as it advances Russia's standing and interests, recovers Russia's reputation as a stable and reliable partner of Iran, is a purely economic deal with no political significance, yet also shows that Moscow can independently defy the United States with impunity (obviously a contradiction here), and can lead to future deals, as Iran has proposed a consortium for joint assembly of nuclear fuel.[157]

Even if we take the termination of the S-300 sale into account, it does not change the analysis. Moscow repeatedly warned Iran that its noncooperation was endangering the sale of the weapon; moreover, it came under substantial pressure from both Israel and the United States, and it was widely believed that selling the S-300 to Iran would trigger an Israeli air strike, the last thing Moscow wants.[158] As we have shown above, the gains it might make from selling the missile were negligible and the costs high, not least the costs of not getting what it wants from Washington. Nonetheless, it has left the door open for future collaboration with Iran on arms sales and other issues if it negotiates with the United States, EU Three, and Russia in a 5 + 1 framework.[159]

Even if this termination of the S-300 enraged Iranian elites, from Moscow's standpoint, the recent energy deals clearly stabilized Russo-Iranian relations while removing Russia from collaboration beyond a certain point with Washington, showing that the "U.S. reset with Russia on Iran is the shakiest leg of its Iran policy."[160] It also suggests that Russia wants to tie the United States down with Iran, while it advances on other fronts and keeps raising the ante for its cooperation as it improves its ties to Iran at U.S. expense.[161] Nonetheless, both Russian and foreign analysts acknowledge that the apparent turn towards restoring or at least restabilizing ties to Iran comes at the expense of the reset policy and could mark its symbolic end.[162] Clearly, the road to Tehran does not lead through Moscow.[163]

Obviously Russia's robust economic interests in Iran and the nuclear, energy, and defense industry lobbies that benefit from those interests greatly influence Moscow's policies. But beyond those lobbies, Russia's fundamental strategic interests lie in promoting Irano-U.S. hostility, not cooperation. Official Russian statements advocate strengthening Iran's role as a legitimate actor in a Middle East security system even as Iranian leaders threaten to destroy Israel and promote state-sponsored terrorism. Foreign Minister Lavrov went beyond this and said that Iran should even be invited to participate in any security system for the Black Sea region![164] Moscow's recent call for a nuclear free Middle East is, in this connection, essentially a propaganda stunt. This call is directed explicitly against Israel, whose assumed nuclear program has never been seen by Middle Eastern governments as a threat requiring them to do anything.[165] However, since Iran's program went into high gear Moscow has offered 13 Arab states nuclear reactors to advance its economic, political, and strategic interests in the Middle East, hardly a contribution to nonproliferation.[166] Indeed, Moscow has been feverishly trying to sell reactors abroad, even to potential proliferators like Myanmar, for years.[167]

For over a decade, Russian pundits and officials have openly stated that they want Iran to be a partner of Russia and not the United States, lest the United States consolidate its position as the leading foreign power in the Middle East, where Moscow still desperately desires to be seen as a great power capable of influencing regional policy. Irano-American hostility precludes such consolidation and permits Russia to exercise influence by supporting the maintenance of a system of controlled tension there. Second, Iranian rapprochement with the West undermines Russia's use of the energy weapon to subvert European security institutions and governments because large quantities of Iranian gas and oil would then be shipped to Europe. An Iranian reorientation to the West would also likely stimulate foreign investment to and access from Central Asia through Iran to the Persian Gulf and the Indian Ocean, allowing the free flow of Central Asian energy to the entire world, bypassing Russia and undermining its ability to control Eurasian energy flows.

Recent Russian statements confirm this assessment. Even though Moscow is quite unhappy with Iranian stonewalling, it refuses to support the idea of extending sanctions, still calls for negotiating with Iran in order to ease the burden of sanctions upon Iran, and rejects "unilateral" (i.e., Western and U.S.) sanctions on Iran. Key figures like Prime Minister Putin and NATO ambassador Dmitry Rogozin deny that Iran has shown signs of having a military nuclear program. Meanwhile, Russia's arms sales agency, Rosoboroneksport, still holds out the possibility of selling nonsanctioned weapons to Iran.[168] While Russo-Iranian relations have eroded due to the sanctions and

Russia's tougher line, formally Iran still holds out, as does Russia, prospects for renewed cooperation. Indeed, though Medvedev calls Iran's policy unreasonably tough and has warned that it is getting closer to producing nuclear weapons, his government seems not to have gotten that message, and even he calls energy cooperation with Iran promising.[169] And Lavrov has added that sanctions have run their course and that "any new proposals would basically be aimed at suffocating the Iranian economy."[170] So presumably Moscow will oppose further sanctions against Iran. In other words, Moscow has again tried to have its cake and eat it too. Therefore, the presumption that we can expect any genuinely serious cooperation from Moscow beyond the present limit regarding Iran that brings Iran to halt its program is unfounded, even mischievous. Certainly we cannot expect that the Russian government will accept any linkage between arms control issues and Iran, as it has already rejected that stance.[171] But we can probably expect linkage to getting America to retreat further in Eurasia, whether it is missile defense or the integration of those borderlands into the West.

Korea.

The other proliferation threat is North Korea. Moscow's regional calculus and effective power to help us here is limited and very different from its role vis-à-vis Iran. Yet it might offer possibilities for the United States to advance its interests, if Washington plays its cards right. Neither Washington nor Moscow has much, if any, leverage over North Korean policy. Indeed, the DPRK possibly could disintegrate from internal failure even as it possesses nuclear weapons or alternatively it could, through miscalculation or deliberate policy, trigger war. Already in September 2010, Russian Deputy Foreign Minister Alexei Borodavkin, Moscow's delegate to the Six-Party Talks, said that the Korean peninsula was on the brink of war, something nobody else has said in public.[172]

Today the Six-Party process is moribund, if not dead. China has made a proposal to resume negotiations first between the two Korean states, followed by a DPRK-U.S. negotiation, and then resumption of the full Six-Party Talks. But Seoul has yet to approve this plan formally or renounce its demand for North Korean apology for sinking its ship (the *Cheonan*) last year or for initiating firing on Yeonpyeong island in November 2010.[173] Most recently, Russian diplomatic observers appeared to pour cold water on any resumption of the Six-Party Talks because of what looks like insuperable divergences between Seoul and Pyongyang that would preclude even their meeting anytime soon.[174] Even before this period, several observers had begun to criticize the Six-Party process for failing to achieve its task, but that criticism has only grown since then.[175] Indeed, Niklas Swanstrom of Sweden's Institute for Development and Policy flatly says the process is dead.[176] This stagnation of the Six-Party process preceded the latest Korean crisis generated by the announcement that North Korea has a uranium enrichment plant much more sophisticated than anyone believed (probably greatly assisted by foreign powers) and North Korea's shelling of the South Korean island of Yeonpyeong in November 2010. But the process' stagnation was visible even before the *Cheonan* incident of March 2010 when North Korea torpedoed a South Korean ship. North Korea is also reportedly preparing a third nuclear test.[177] Since previous tests have led to ruptures in the process and to UN resolutions imposing sanctions on North Korea (which apparently surprised Pyongyang), another test, especially in the current climate, will likely further delay if not kill the resumption of Six-Party Talks.

While many reasons exist for this stagnation, because of this apparent breakdown of the process all these reasons have combined to bring about the growing intransigence of the major parties. Indeed, China's aforementioned proposal reflects the inutility of previous structures like the Six-Party process. This intransigence strongly suggests that, absent a major change in one of the key participants' policies, no change is in sight even though continuation of this impasse promises no relief of the current crisis for any of the six parties. But without major changes, the next crisis is liable to be much more dangerous, as South Korea has now publicly announced that it will retaliate in force against new attacks.[178] And the advent of this uranium enrichment plant opens up the possibility for North Korea to begin building many more nuclear bombs.[179]

Thus there is good reason for mounting concern. North Korea, too, now talks of the situation as being on the brink of war, and South Korea has pledged retaliation for any future Northern provocations.[180] The current crisis reminds us of the dangers that are constantly present in the area and of the many reasons for vigilance regarding North Korea. Even though the succession of Kim Jong Un has so far progressed without incident, we cannot take the enduring stability of North Korea for granted.

This is more than the habitual warning of many observers that North Korea will or should collapse. Many signs point to a genuine possibility of internal ferment within North Korea even apart from a possible succession crisis. The outbreak of a major domestic crisis, whether or not it is tied to foreign challenges, could destabilize North Korea and lead to very grave and unforeseen crises.[181] For example, while many argue that incidents like the *Cheonan* affair may be driven by the exigencies of the succession issue in North Korean politics, i.e., the need to elicit military support for the heir; succession to Kim Jong-Il, as many experts know, could quite easily trigger internal and/or external clashes in and around the DPRK that could easily drag the outside powers into conflict, and North Korean military risk taking on this scale ranks high among those possible contingencies.[182] In addition, many signs point to a genuine possibility of internal ferment within North Korea even apart from the succession crisis.

All this occurs in the context of the apparent ascendancy of North Korean hardliners and the military. Given the looming succession crisis and inflation, along with this ascendancy of anti-reform and pronuclear elements, this hardening policy line undermines prospects for a more accommodating foreign policy even if Pyongyang returns to the Six-Party Talks. Beyond the regime's efforts to clamp down at home lies the fact that many indicators point to what Soviet historians might have called a revolutionary crisis in North Korean society. Defections, corruption, riots when the 2009 currency reform was introduced, jailbreaks, the breaking of the regime's information monopoly, and a precarious food situation are all hallmarks of a potential that could erupt if there is a break in leadership or elite cohesion. Alternatively, elites who lose out may defect or seek to overturn that result. Indeed, the United States and the Republic of Korea (ROK) have already confidentially discussed unification scenarios.[183] Meanwhile, the present impact of these trends that commingle decline and domestic hardening undermines prospects for a more accommodating foreign policy even if Pyongyang returns to the Six-Party Talks.

Second, foreign discussions concerning Pyongyang's motives for precipitating the crises of 2010 also are deeply disturbing. The many media commentaries attempting to ascertain North Korea's motives usually divide into the following explanations, some of which may overlap as being multiple causes for its behavior. Analyses focusing on domestic determinants of the DPRK's actions claim that that the regime is acting because it needs to get the military's support for Kim Jong Un in the current succession. The price for this support is to conduct aggressive moves against the United States and South Korea and demonstrate, e.g., through the enrichment facility, that North Korea will never renounce nuclear weapons.[184] That denouement, in turn, vitiates any prospect for resuming the Six-Party Talks because from Washington's, if not Tokyo's and Seoul's, viewpoints, this North Korean stance means there is nothing to talk about in these negotiations.

The assessments that emphasize foreign policy drivers claim (and there is no necessary contradiction between them and the analyses stressing domestic factors) that North Korea is employing its habitual tactics to force the United States to take it seriously and engage it in bilateral negotiations and possibly also is simultaneously trying to induce South Korea to restore elements, if not all, of the Sunshine Policy and economic transfers to the North.[185] While it is impossible to determine conclusively which of these analyses of the DPRK's motives is correct, and what is the primary driver of North Korea's actions, the conclusions that can be drawn from these assessments are extremely disturbing. North Korea has continued not just to develop nuclear weapons, but also to conduct a highly risk acceptant policy. This risk acceptant policy is not merely illustrated in the three provocations of 2010 but in its transfer of missiles and proliferation capabilities abroad. Such policies also include the sale of nuclear reactors to Syria and missiles to proliferators. Indeed, by 2007 North Korea had established itself as, "the Third World's greatest supplier of missiles, missile components and related technologies."[186] U.S. diplomats also believe that North Korea furnished Iran with 19 missiles based on a Russian design for submarine based missiles called R-27 that North Korea calls BM-25 missiles. These nuclear capable missiles enable Iran to reach European capitals including Moscow.[187] But they also allow the DPRK to attack much further into Asia or the Pacific than has hitherto been believed.

North Korea's risk-acceptant behavior appears to be premised on the belief that not only will Russia and China ultimately restrain the United States from imposing truly serious punishments (be they sanctions or worse) upon North Korea, but that the United States will be unable or unwilling to use its full power to strike back at North Korea for these risky moves. Neither will Russia or China be able to exercise any decisive restraining leverage upon North Korea. Therefore, North Korea can behave provocatively at what it believes to be a minimum or at least manageable risk. While this behavior has allowed North Korea to get nuclear weapons without paying what it considers to be an unbearable price, it also exposes its supposed "backers" to the consequences of these great risks taken in disregard of their interests and without their knowledge or acceptance of the risks for them in that behavior.[188] Yet until now, Russian and Chinese behavior has allowed North Korea to keep on behaving in this provocative manner. As a result, North Korea has repeatedly been able to outmaneuver the other five members of the process to the point where U.S. officials have publicly charged that China's refusal to exercise a decisive restraining pressure upon the DPRK, in fact, means that China has become North Korea's enabler, a charge that rankles China deeply.[189] China may have retracted its position somewhat in trying to induce a return to some agreeable forum for negotiations. But it is quite unlikely that in the present configuration, North Korea will renounce its nuclear weapons. Its demands that the United States cease its "hostile policy" essentially amount to an abandonment of South Korea, not denuclearization.[190]

Yet, as of now nothing seems likely to alter Pyongyang's calculation of the costs it incurs by acting this way, including the most recent crises. Indeed, at least some Russian experts believe that it is impossible to scare North Korea with sanctions.[191] In that case, what then can the other parties do to it, especially if Beijing stands behind it as seems to be the case now? Furthermore, in conjunction with the likelihood that further incidents along the lines of the *Cheonan* incident might be in the offing, this kind of behavior could easily ignite the conflagration that Moscow, if not other capitals, most fear.

Under the circumstances, the fact that the military appears to be the strongest faction in North Korean politics, and one that must be appeased by provocative international behavior to cement the succession, or even, as some analysts suggest, that it may to some degree be acting on its own, raises many great threats to regional security.[192] If aggressive and defiant international behavior is the price of legitimacy at home, we can expect many more crises, especially as North Korea has long acted on the belief that the only way to get Washington's or Seoul's attention is to create a major crisis, and it may well believe it can take risks with impunity. But under present conditions, the domestic politics of the United States and South Korea (as well as probably Japan) preclude any generosity on their part to North Korea or quick return to the six-party talks absent guarantees of denuclearization and an end to provocations, which are no less impossible for North Korea to give due to its domestic politics. Indeed, so far the United States, Japan, and South Korea have, not unexpectedly, been unwilling to return to the talks without apologies for *Cheonan* or guarantees of denuclearization.[193]

Consequently, the intersection of the main players' domestic politics and regional threat perceptions work together to frustrate anything but a deepening cycle of provocations and resistance. Equally plausible is the fact that North Korean leaders may think they can take greater risks than are warranted and miscalculate the outcome. A similar danger may occur in the United States and South Korean governments if their domestic politics make it impossible for them to ignore further North Korean provocations. In either case, it is pretty clear that in fact nobody can truly control North Korea's behavior or is willing to. Russia certainly has no leverage on it, and China's attitude has been less than helpful from Washington's point of view.[194]

Likewise, there is no reason to believe that this risk-acceptant and provocative behavior will stop even if new sanctions are imposed. First of all, North Korea needs the revenues it gains from proliferation, which are vital to its economic survival. Second, as many analysts have argued, China remains unwilling to bring to bear its full weight to truly implement the existing UN imposed sanctions. So, new sanctions cannot achieve much in any case.[195] More sanctions, even if they are passed by the UN, only make it harder to return to the Six-Party process, and not only because we cannot really count on their full implementation. Since North Korea demands an end to sanctions that ban its arms trade as a precondition of returning to the talks, any new sanctions probably only strengthen its resolve not to rejoin the process. Meanwhile, North Korea clearly intends to continue these missile sales despite UN resolutions and other international mechanisms to block them, such as the Proliferation Security Initiative. If such blatant risk taking continues unabated, there are real chances that Pyongyang could miscalculate its adversaries' response and end up with a much greater crisis than it had bargained for.

Beyond this assessment, Michael O'Hanlon has identified a series of other dangers that could easily grow out of the current situation on the Korean peninsula. These are the dangers of proliferation either to terrorists or other states. In the case of collapse, control over nuclear materials could easily deteriorate, enabling possessors of those materials to sell them abroad to the highest bidder. On the other hand, should North Korea keep on going as a nuclear power, its capabilities could either weaken deterrence among the members of the U.S. Asian alliance system, or even start a war entailing missile strikes on South Korea, Japan, or even possibly the United States. Lastly, a nuclear North Korea could engender a "nuclear domino effect," leading Japan, South Korea, and possibly other states to contemplate going, or to actually go, nuclear.[196]

The primary causes for the present situation reside first in the fundamental incompatibility of the DPRK and U.S. positions; second, in some of the inherent problems of the Six-Party mechanism; third, in the evolving disparities in the positions of the participants; and fourth in the greatly transformed Asian strategic environment since 2003 when the talks began. While North Korea now says it is prepared to return to the talks, it also states that it will not give up its nuclear weapons under any conditions. Indeed, it has been saying this since 2009, if not earlier.[197] It is likely that this remains the case, suggesting that the U.S. demand for an irrevocable prior commitment to complete, verifiable, and irreversible disarmament (CVID) of its nuclear weapons (the old Bush policy) is a nonstarter and thus an exercise in futility. Indeed, analysts like the Russian Korea expert, Georgy Toloraya, have openly argued that if the talks are about denuclearization first and other issues subsequently, then they will be futile, as North Korea will simply refuse to play a serious part.[198]

According to Toloraya:

> The usefulness of the Six Party Talks seems to North Koreans to have been exhausted. Further down the road they would have to discuss — and probably be pressed for concessions on something really tangible, such as their reprocessed fissile materials and actual nuclear weapons. That, most likely, formed no part of their calculations, at least at the early stage of searching for a strategic compromise with the West. Understandably, North Koreans became frustrated, as their tangible gains from the multiparty process were marginal. They did not come much closer to getting sub-

stantial security guarantees, and even the largely symbolic (and easily reversible) "delisting" of the DPRK as a terrorist state caused much controversy in the US and elsewhere, and led to demands for new concessions from it in return. North Koreans saw that as a breach of trust. Modest economic assistance was indeed promised when the accord was sealed, but only Russia carried out its obligations (200 thousand tons of heavy oil), while other countries either totally abstained (Japan) or dragged their feet. The DPRK felt that its concessions were not fully recognized and valued. "Hawks" in Pyongyang might also have suspected that concessions were perceived in the West as a sign of weakness and testimony to their pressing need to normalize relations. No one was impressed, at least to the extent that North Koreans had probably expected, with the actual opening of its nuclear program and even the disabling of some objects, though such things were unimaginable just a few years ago.[199]

Thus Pyongyang has announced that its agenda for resuming negotiations focuses on the following clear set of goals;

- Recognition of its status as a de facto nuclear weapon state or, failing that, preventing efforts to disarm its nuclear weapons,
- Convincing Washington and others that they have no choice but to normalize relations with North Korea as a nuclear state,
- Maximizing all the material benefits to be gained through negotiations while conceding nothing on its nuclear program,
- Convincing the international community and UNSC to lift existing sanctions and impose no new ones,
- Shifting discussion of the Six-Party Talks from denuclearization to a "peace regime" based on

ending or attenuating the U.S. alliances with Japan and South Korea.[200]

Consequently, its conditions for rejoining the process are completely antithetical to the U.S. position that demands an advance commitment, much like the Bush administration did to complete, verifiable, and irreversible nuclear disarmament and has shown no interest in a preceding peace settlement. Pyongyang's demands and defiant assertion that it will not denuclearize therefore run straight into Washington's counter demand that it will not recognize the DPRK as a nuclear weapons state, and that it must reenter the negotiations without any preconditions and denuclearize to avoid further sanctions. Indeed, even China agrees that a peace treaty to the Korean War cannot be signed until the North denuclearizes.[201] Thus at best, an impasse appears to be the foreseeable future of the Six-Party process, even if it somehow resumed soon.

This impasse alone could suffice to torpedo any early resumption of the Six-Party process. But in the context of the added crises of November 2010, the domestic constraints on key actors in the wake of U.S. elections, the collapse of the Sunshine Policy, North Korea's succession, and the recent attacks and provocations against the South, it is difficult to see the point of resuming them, let alone how this resumption might come about. Yet under the circumstances the stagnation of the Six-Party process could quite conceivably lead to renewed crises, especially as North Korea thinks it has to provoke ever-new crises to get its views heard. Indeed, the Six-Party process has functioned until now largely as a mechanism for crisis management. But clearly the process is not working or managing crises and could break down. This is not altogether surprising inasmuch as the process has contained within it the seeds of such an outcome from its inception.

A second cause for the failure of the talks lies in the inherent practical and theoretical difficulties in arranging any truly coherent multilateral consensus, let alone a unity of views and actions on an issue touching on all six participants' vital national interests.[202] Inasmuch as all efforts to make progress on or even resolve the North Korean issues take place within an environment of multiple triangular and bilateral relationships among the participants, the problems of mutual coordination are inherently very difficult.[203] Beyond these considerations, the record of multilateral security institutions in Asia is not particularly encouraging. Michael Wesley points out that multilateral Asian security institutions have done poorly in adapting their original function to changing power realities, notably rising powers' demands, and in any case the Six-Party process has yet to become an accepted multilateral security organization rather than a crisis management or a somewhat ad hoc organization.[204] Indeed, the abundant evidence of the competitive approaches of the six parties to regional security in Northeast Asia, particularly in the now dynamic evolution of this region with a rising China, a seemingly declining America, and a threatening North Korea, underscores the difficulty in using the Six-Party process to find a multilateral harmony over the issues on its agenda.[205]

Third, now there is an added problem of emerging different conceptions of what the Six-Party process is supposed to achieve. China, for example, is retreating from the idea that the talks should aim to denuclearize North Korea and serve rather as a means to reduce tensions. When Kim Jong-Il visited China in August 2010, the Chinese press and Kim Jong-Il both stressed that the purpose of the talks was to reduce or even prevent tensions on the peninsula, not arrange for denuclearization or a peace treaty for the Korean War.[206] If this concept of the talks is allowed to gain credence, North Korea will become a nuclear state de facto and possibly de jure but will remain an outlaw state in many real ways and thus an obstacle rather than a contributor to regional security because the United States, ROK, and Japan will not currently accept North Korea as a nuclear state. Nor will they accept upending the Six-Party Talks to serve an agenda that only benefits Beijing and Pyongyang at their expense.

Even if Russia and China are correct to argue that denuclearization can only come about as a result of a long-term process of confidence-building and mutual security guarantees, Washington, Seoul, and Tokyo were in no mood to hear this argument even before November 2010 and the events of that month. Since then, North Korean generated crises and the U.S. elections virtually preclude any movement to meet Beijing and Moscow, let alone Pyongyang, halfway. Japan has publicly stated its belief that this is not an auspicious time to reconvene the talks, and South Korea and Washington agree with this. South Korea is demanding an apology for the recent shelling of Yeonpyeong, and the United States still insists on a prior commitment to denuclearization as a precondition for resuming the Six-Party Talks.[207]

Since the end of 2010, this apparent breakdown of the process due to all these reasons has fostered the growing intransigence of the major parties. Thus there is good reason for mounting concern. This intransigence strongly suggests that, absent a major change in one of the key participants' policies, no change is in sight even though continuation of this impasse promises no relief of the current crisis for any of the six parties. Without major changes, the next crisis is liable to be much more dangerous, as South Korea has now publicly announced that it will retaliate in force against new attacks.[208] And, as noted above, the advent of the uranium enrichment plant opens up the possibility for North Korea to begin building many more nuclear bombs.[209] In addition, North Korea now talks of the situation as being on the brink of war, and South Korea has pledged retaliation for any future Northern provocations.[210] More recently, it was reported that South Korea might gain support from the United States to lengthen the reach of its missiles and is exploring options for returning U.S. TNW to South Korea. While this was denied, there are political figures in the ROK who now openly advocate returning those missiles that were removed with the end of the Cold War in 1991.[211]

THREATS TO RUSSIA

The threats from further impasse or deterioration of the Korean situation to Russia are numerous and underappreciated in the West. For example, since the *Cheonan* incident in 2010, the United States has sought more options with which to punish North Korea, even if it does not seek war against it. That incident also has led South Korea to consult even more closely with both the United States and Japan on a coordinated response, thereby marginalizing Russia and isolating China.[212] Beyond that, the fallout from this incident forced Russia to enter into very intense and close consultations with China even though it has no real influence over the other actors.[213] But because both China and Russia share the view that the greater danger is instability on the Korean peninsula, China failed to act this time against North Korea; it and Russia have been in some measure isolated, while the United States and its allies have grown closer and more demanding. They are still in no hurry to resume the Six-Party process without prior North Korean concessions.[214] Not only does this isolate China and Russia, it also deprives Russia of its minimal means of influencing regional events and preserves the regional bipolarity in Northeast Asia that could more easily lead to a conflict against its interests. Asian observers even believe that China's failure to act contributed to Washington's decision to move naval vessels closer to China.[215] We could therefore see more provocative behavior from North Korea and a hardening of U.S. positions that would merely intensify the existing polarization between Washington and Pyongyang, as well as that between Washington and Beijing, and increase mistrust, suspicion, etc.

The current situation also offers other dangers to Russia, e.g., marginalization. Clearly, nobody has considered it seriously as a partner in the diplomacy revolving around this crisis. South Korea and the United States approached China and Japan to coordinate regional and allied responses, isolating Russia even though China failed to act. Consequently, Russia unilaterally stepped into the breach, conducting its own investigation of the incident and desperately scrambling to save the Six-Party process or figure out some other process through which it can play a role commensurate with its ambitions. The Russian investigation challenged South Korea's view, saying the ship sank due to an explosion caused by its own navigational errors, but this investigation was not released, lest Russia's position be further eroded.[216]

Whatever problems these trends cause for the other five powers, arguably this impasse most injures Russia as a participant in the larger Korean peace process. Since this process not only aims to deal with the DPRK's nuclear proliferation, but also to chart a path toward an overall peace for Korea and to create new multilateral frameworks for Northeast Asia, the longer this impasse lasts, the more Russia suffers. This is not just because Russia is the chairman of the working group on a new multilateral security system for Northeast Asia, although that is serious enough. The current impasse threatens Russian interests in many ways. First, Russia confronts an explosive situation and potential crisis of immense magnitude on its doorstep where it has little or no influence over many of the main actors, not least Pyongyang. This crisis, which it can do little to manage or control, has enormous potential consequences for Russia. A recent article in the Ministry of Foreign Affairs' journal, *International Affairs*, stated (incidentally quoting a Chinese analyst, Zhou Feng):

> Indeed, the situation on the Korean Peninsula, which is in close proximity to our Far Eastern borders, is explosive and fraught with the most unpredictable consequences. Peace is very fragile here. No one can guarantee that it will not collapse as a result of a clash between the two Koreas with the involvement of other countries in the conflict and the use of weapons of mass destruction. "The aggravation of the North Korean nuclear issue is one of the long standing problems leading to new ones. This issue cannot be expected to be settled easily because difficulties have emerged in relations among large East Asian states. The settlement process can subsequently lead to a redistribution of roles of large states on the Asian political field — that is a new regional security problem.[217]

That restructuring of the Asian political order could easily ensue at Russia's expense, given its visibly relative weakness there, and it could ensue by means over which Russia has little or no influence, even if they are not violent means. While Moscow has long since said that it does not fear the unification of the two Koreas and might actually welcome that outcome, it could only do so if it happened through a peaceful process, not war.[218]

This potential restructuring of the Asian state system also has profound implications for RFE that Moscow already sees as a major security problem due to its relative poverty, isolation from European Russia, and vulnerability to a host of foreign influences, particularly a Chinese economic takeover.[219] Failure to move forward on the Korean issues, if it leads to war or the stagnation of regional economic development, threatens Russia's domestic development program for the RFE. As Gleb Ivashentsov, Moscow's Ambassador to Seoul has said:

> In no other region are internal and external interests of Russia so interconnected as in Northeast Asia. For the future of Russia as a great power to a great extent depends on the economic, technological, and social uplift of Siberia and the Russian Far East. To achieve that aim we need the absence of external threats. By Russia's view such guarantees could be best provided by promoting positive relations with her neighbors.[220]

Therefore Russia desperately wants to prevent a war breaking out over Korea either by U.S. and ROK attacks upon the North, or if the North was to attack South Korea or Japan. Moscow's reaction to the *Cheonan* incident, its professed skepticism as to whether North Korea actually sank the ship, insistence on conducting its own investigation, readiness to cooperate with China to avert escalation of the crisis by all means, and insistence on returning to the table all indicate its anxiety lest this crisis engender a breakdown of the negotiation process or actual conflict.[221]

That conflict could quickly escalate even to the nuclear level and only end with a hostile power (either the United States or China) occupying North Korea and its border with Russia. It is not certain that Russia could stay out of such a war, and the consequences for it would, under almost every imaginable circumstance, be very severe. No outcome here is acceptable to Russia, but its means of preventing these possible outcomes are decidedly limited. At the same time, conflict in the Korean peninsula also undermines any hope of developing the RFE with foreign assistance, since Russia cannot do so alone. Absent such development all talk of Russia as a great Asian power remains just that, talk.

Beyond preventing a war Russia has several other objectives regarding Korea that are now at risk due to the current impasse. Primarily, it seeks to obtain lasting acknowledgement of its status as a great Asian power that can participate in and is necessary for establishing a regional Asian-Pacific security system. Indeed, it publicly regards its participation in these talks as a touchstone of the international recognition and acknowledgment of that status. Therefore, it takes its standing in the Six-Party process very seriously. Russia's exclusion from the efforts in the 1990s to deal with North Korea's nuclearization were widely resented and taken as a sign of its marginality in Asia, much to Russia's anger. Prominent U.S. Asia expert Lowell Dittmer actually referred to the Russia of this time as a diplomatic nonentity.[222] Not surprisingly, foreign, if

71

not domestic, observers also seriously questioned the notion that Russia was a great power or entitled to claim such a status that every Russian politician believes to be Russia's birthright.[223]

Moreover, continuing impasse prevents Russia from recovering any true economic influence as a large-scale energy provider to both Koreas and essentially cedes the field to China, if not other players, as states who might gain economic influence over North Korea. Moscow intends to use its ability to supply both Koreas with energy both to ensure its place in the settlement, and unite them with Russia in an enduring economic-political association. Once the Six-Party agreement of February 2007 took shape, *ITAR-TASS* reported comments by a foreign policy expert that Russia could create the conditions needed to implement "a series of major multilateral projects with the participation of both North Korea and Russia," including oil and gas transit, electricity transfers, and the so-called TKR-TSR project connecting a Trans-Korean railway with Russia's Trans-Siberian railway, the centerpiece of Russian transport policy for Asia.[224] Significantly, this source saw these projects as benefiting not just Moscow and Pyongyang, but also Seoul.[225]

Both the ROK and Russia also eagerly wish to construct a Russian gas pipeline through both Koreas, complete with a petrochemical industrial park and a LNG plant. That should begin in 2010, be completed in 2015, and ship 7.5 million tons of gas (measured in LNG) annually for 30 years, 20 percent of the ROK's annual import of natural gas.[226] The cost of this so-called natural gas pipeline (PNG) project is enormous.

> If it succeeds, this will be a super-size economic cooperation project worth over $100 US Billion, covering

the purchasing price of natural gas (US $90 Billion), construction costs for the petrochemical industrial park (US$ 9 Billion), and construction costs for the PNG through North Korea. (US$3 Billion) This project will represent a typical energy development project promoted by the Lee-Myung Bak government.[227]

The opportunity to provide North Korea, and through it South Korea, with reliable sources of energy is essential if Russia is to be a meaningful presence in the Korean peninsula and Northeast Asia's regional security order. Indeed, energy supplies might be the only way Russia can play a major role in any Korean peace process. Even that might not be enough as we have seen how little Russia actually contributes to the Six-Party Talks. In 2007-08, there was even speculation that Russia is wearying of the Six-Party Talks due both to North Korea's obstreperous behavior but also because the bilateral talks between the United States and North Korea had sidelined it and Japan, relegating them to a lower status in the talks.[228] In the Russo-Japanese foreign ministers talks in December 2009, Foreign Minister Lavrov dismissed such talk, paradoxically and unintentionally suggesting Russia's fears of any bilateral U.S.-DPRK deal.[229] Naturally, Russian analysts are at pains to refute such arguments, constantly invoking Russia's importance to the talks, its constructive plans for a settlement, etc.[230] Nevertheless despite its rancor at these characterizations, the fact remains that Russia is far from being a major factor at these talks whereas the United States and China are the players whose role is decisive to their outcome. Consequently, the collapse of the Six-Party process is a major loss for Russia because it delays and minimizes Russia's chances to count for something serious in the Korean security equation and puts its overall

Asian policy at considerable risk. Not surprisingly, it has consistently counseled moderation towards North Korea, been very cautious about sanctions even though President Medvedev considers North Korea a greater threat than Iran, and has steadfastly argued for resuming the Six-Party Talks despite North Korea's provocative nuclear and missile tests. Moscow has steadily argued against military action, hinted that sanctions might be lifted if the DPRK rejoined the talks, suggested that the IAEA become involved with this issue, and proclaimed its willingness to provide economic assistance.[231] But it is Washington and Beijing, not Moscow, that will decide the issue of the talks for Pyongyang, signifying Russia's limited power to influence events here.

The breakdown of those talks also nullifies the discussions that Moscow sponsored about creating a multilateral security mechanism for Northeast Asia as part of the 2007 agreements, a long-standing point in Soviet and Russian foreign policy.[232] As Georgy Toloraya writes:

> Russia sees a multiparty diplomatic process as essential for attaining the aforementioned objectives. The eventual creation of a regional (or sub-regional) system of security and cooperation in Northeast Asia would benefit Russia, as it would enable it to have a greater say in the area and create more opportunities to promote its own interests, including economic ones. Russia aspires to become a "Eurasian bridge" which would speed up the development of its Far Eastern regions and facilitate its deeper integration in the Asian economic space, and its development as an "Asian energy-power."[233]

Absent such a mechanism, Moscow finds it harder to play a role in Northeast Asia as an independent competitive actor. Nonetheless, Moscow keeps devising formulas for regional conflict resolution because it now publicly admits to anxiety about the future security equation. Deputy Foreign Minister Alexei Borodavkin, Moscow's representative to the Six-Party Talks, announced that Russia's discussions with the other five parties led it to formulate a draft on "Guiding Principles for Peace and Security in Northeast Asia." Borodavkin admitted that existing conflicts in Korea and Afghanistan worsened in 2009. Consequently, "We proceed from the assumption that one of the most important prerequisites and components of the denuclearization process is the formation of regional common security institutions which would be based on the principle of equal security to all parties."[234] Such calls underscore Moscow's less than equal status here that makes the success of such plans unlikely. But Borodavkin further underscored Russia's genuine alarm about Korea by stating that the aggravation of Asian conflicts, together with the global economic crisis have created a situation where, "Under current circumstances, peace, and security in the region is a priority task because we believe that neither nuclear deterrence nor military deterrence may ensure security in this sub-region and in the entire world."[235] That is, further North Korean provocations might push one or another actor over the edge, and Russia cannot do anything to stop it. Indeed, Moscow even deployed its new S-400 SAM to the RFE from fears that North Korea might launch more missiles that either go awry or worse, provoke a major conflict in Northeast Asia.[236] For Borodavkin, this danger means Russia must participate more actively in the region, and its activity has become more substantive, focused on economic inte-gration.[237]

Thus even though Moscow has indicated its will-ingness as part of the reset policy to cooperate with Washington on curbing proliferation, it has a very different posture and outlook regarding the two most outstanding proliferation issues currently on the in-ternational agenda. If the reset policy is not to be un-done due to the confluence of regional security and proliferation issues that challenge both sides' ability to find common ground, something more is needed. Or to put it bluntly, the U.S. policy of "strategic pa-tience" in regard to North Korea, which boils down to making no moves until Pyongyang concedes to Wash-ington's agenda, must be amended, if not reversed. In Iran's case, too, something must be done because Iran, despite foreign pressures, and the U.S. effort at engaging it, shows no sign of slowing down or re-nouncing its quest for nuclear weapons. In the Iranian case, while some have argued that the United States should accept deterrence of a nuclear Iran our allies, particularly Israel and Saudi Arabia, cannot and will not accept that strategy. For them, a nuclear Iran is an existential threat of the highest order and an intel-ligent approach will realize that Iran cannot therefore (especially given the current turmoil in the Middle East) be allowed to gain usable nuclear weapons un-der any circumstances.

POLICY RECOMMENDATIONS

A sound U.S. policy approach that considers the regional dimensions of the reset policy, as well as the limited utility to date of Russian cooperation on pro-liferation issues, should understand that more of the same, especially in Korea, is an abdication of responsibility, not an answer to the problems confronting any U.S. administration's efforts to advance the national interest. In plain English, the U.S. 20-year obsession with proliferation has led to a virtually complete strategic and policy failure. Far from reducing it, we are, in fact, managing proliferation. India and Pakistan have gone nuclear, other nuclear powers are modernizing their arsenals, nothing has stopped Iran, the war in Iraq to terminate its alleged proliferation was a disaster, and North Korea has nuclear weapons and is testing nuclear weapons of ever greater range and capability. As one recent account observes:

> Despite many rhetorical compliments, the Six-Party Talks have revealed their limit as a framework to resolve the North Korean nuclear crisis. North Korea quadrupled nuclear capabilities during the talks, conducted two nuclear tests, built up uranium enrichment capabilities and secretly provided Syria with an upgraded version of the 5MWEe reactor at Yongbyon. Compared to the mid-1990s, the amount of plutonium the DPRK possesses has increased form 7-12.5kg to 28.5-49 kg at the end of 2007. The possible number of nuclear warheads has also increased from 1-5 to 5-20 or so depending on various criteria and technologies. This is the end result of the Six-Party Talks.[238]

It also appears that in both Iran and North Korea's cases, they can still count on Moscow and Beijing to mitigate any sanctions policy and obstruct the outcome of any diplomatic pressure on them to yield nuclear weapons as part of a political process. Furthermore, in the wake of current trends in the Middle East, it appears that the U.S. position and perception of its reliability are eroding. In the Far East, if we look at the Russian position in a perspective that includes the situation on the Korean peninsula, mounting concern is also warranted. Though Russia has been a vital player in Asia since the 1858 treaty of Aigun with China if not earlier, Russian and foreign observers acknowledge that in East Asia, it confronts marginalization as a significant, not to mention great, power. Confirming this bleak assessment and expanding it is the shocking (at least it should be shocking to Moscow and other observers) fact cited by a U.S. Army colonel who leads officers on tours of Asian think tanks that Chinese, Japanese, South Korean, and Mongolian think tanks unanimously told his group in 2010 that Russia would soon play no role in East Asian security.[239] While Russia has essentially had to mortgage the development of the RFE to China because of its own systemic failures, at the same time there is ample evidence that its military increasingly vocally and publicly perceives a mounting Chinese military threat in addition to the potential of China's economy to subordinate Russia to its ambitions. In short, in the larger Asian arena of which the Korean question is a major, but not exclusive, part, Russia confronts the genuine prospect and threat of its marginalization as an independent sovereign, great power actor. That is a nightmare scenario for Russia, yet it appears incapable of doing what is needed to reverse that trend.[240]

The United States will not benefit from that outcome, but China will. Indeed, this trend completes the strategic reversal in Asia that has negated the fundamental strategic principles of U.S. policy there going back to the Open Door Notes of 1898. We no longer have a Russo-Japanese contest of hegemony in Asia in rivalry to the United States, with the prize being domination of China. China's rise transforms the regional, if not global, equation and forces new approaches to regional security issues upon us. Moreover, Russia's failure to develop on its own or to escape the condition its leaders now perceive of being isolated from everyone in Asia only redounds to China's benefit and jeopardizes the overall balance or equilibrium in East Asia.[241]

Historically it was the United States, not China, that defined the parameters of Russian power in Asia. In that context, the satellization of Russia is a blow to a strategy that has lasted since 1898 when John Hay formulated the Open Door policy. Allowing China to usurp that role and downgrade Russia as a factor in Asia signifies our strategic fecklessness. Washington assumed its role beginning in 1898 with the proclamation of the Open Door policy. In 1905 Theodore Roosevelt mediated the Portsmouth Treaty that ended the Russo-Japanese war. The Washington Conference of 1921 redefined the new post-World War I status quo in East Asia and strove to limit the reach of Soviet and Japanese revisionism in China.[242] Franklin Delano Roosevelt's recognition of the Union of Soviet Socialist Republics (USSR) in 1933 was clearly a measure to balance Japan, which had broken that balance, by raising the specter of amity with the Soviet Union, and was understood as such by the USSR, which was gravely threatened by Japanese imperialism.[243] Likewise, Soviet participation in the Pacific War in 1945 was only possible through massive U.S. logistical assistance to Moscow that enabled it to move its forces from Central Europe to the RFE and then into Manchuria, Mongolia, and Korea. Similarly, it was U.S. forces that stopped the North Korean and Chinese offensives in the Korean War, and then subsequently engineered the conversion of China into an American partner and the Sino-Japanese treaty of 1978 that stopped aggressive Soviet policies in East Asia.

Thus Washington upheld first a regional and then simultaneously a global balance until the 1990s, when it began to forget its history. Geopolitically, the strategy rested on upholding Chinese independence against all imperialisms (the open door) keeping Japan and Russia separated and hostile, and preventing or at least containing any Sino-Russian alliance or domination of either one by the other. Hence, our continuing support for Japan's position regarding the Kurile Islands.[244] Accordingly, some of our leading experts have warned that the greatest possible threat facing Washington could be a Sino-Russian alliance. Therefore, signs of such an alliance must be disquieting as this collusion could also betoken the first tangible and successful example of regional balancing against U.S. preponderance.[245] Indeed, adding to our disarray is the fact that we have completely neglected Russia as a potential partner in Asia, even as the reset policy openly stated the need for such partnerships in Europe, the Middle East, and Central Asia. Meanwhile, Russia returned the favor by refusing to discuss its Asian policy and threats to its security with the West.[246]

Given the now visible strategic linkage between the reset policy, Asia's strategic transformation, and the urgency of North Korean proliferation, we have the means and motive to revive our well-conceived strategic tradition since China is intent on defending North Korea and blocking the United States there, and the U.S. military strategy now accepts Russia as a potential partner in East Asia.[247] Moreover, the Russian press, and therefore the Russian government, have noticed that acceptance too.[248] But to implement this strategy, we, our allies, and Russia must take coordinated and reciprocal steps. A strategy based on Chinese weakness is inconceivable. The clear and present danger is not a Russian-Chinese alliance, but rather a Chinese-dominated partnership with Russia and North Korea as junior partners that menace an increasingly apprehensive Japan and South Korea. This generates the need for prior agreement on the basis of intense consultations with Japan and South Korea on vital issues facing them. First, the United States must formulate an initiative towards Russia that helps bring it over to the U.S. side in the Six-Party Talks on Korea. This entails the much greater U.S. engagement with Pyongyang that the DPRK wants. While conservatives and Republicans will oppose this, their policy of isolating North Korea has failed principally because the DPRK can count on Sino-Russian policy to reduce any cost to Pyongyang or its provocative behavior. Ultimately, there is no way out of this issue except by a negotiated settlement or war as we cannot simply count on North Korea yielding to pressure or collapsing. In any case, China blocks and mitigates any successful employment of pressure upon the DPRK, and Russia supports it for now.

Here we must remember that this process is not merely about North Korean disarmament. Rather it is about creating a new, legitimate, and enduring, peaceful order in Northeast Asia in which all the parties can participate securely. Even if we believe or know for sure that North Korea will collapse, we must treat it as if it is a durable and ultimately legitimate state capable of making and implementing commitments made to other players. The notion that we do not negotiate with "evil," while popular, contradicts any notion of sound diplomacy aimed at preventing war, possibly the greatest evil in world politics. Moreover, the earlier widespread belief that North Korea's collapse is only a matter of time has not been borne out.

Despite withering crises, the regime has survived and is currently undergoing a succession transition. While its leadership transition may be a major source of its provocative behavior, it is also clear that no external source has much influence over it, thus North Korea has gained a certain measure of stability. Moreover, its possession of nuclear weapons increases its interlocutors' interest in its stability, not its disintegration. Likewise, the idea that China will exercise pressure on our behalf on North Korea is another unsound idea that has failed to materialize. Therefore, Washington should seek to reshape the East Asian order that would duly emerge there to its advantage and not Beijing's. Absent a coherent or viable allied approach, North Korea will end up as China's economic protectorate as will Russia's Asian provinces, thus undermining any hopes for stability in Northeast Asia for a long time. This logic reinforces our prior point that we cannot count on a North Korean collapse and must seriously engage it.

Meanwhile, Russia benefits greatly by having an American option with which to counter China and while it would not be an ally or even a full partner with us, that offer could appreciably distance it from its lockstep identification with China's Korea policy. For example, a U.S. guarantee that it and/or its allies will underwrite the cost of providing North Korea with Russian energy as part of any subsequent accord would certainly play very well in Moscow. Such an initiative might also make North Korea sit up and take notice that 3+3 bipolarity in the talks had changed to 4+2 against it, where China does not relish being left alone with North Korea. Moreover, only direct engagement with North Korea allows the United States to shape the future of the two Korean states in positive ways without leaving the field to a Russo-Chinese alliance dominated by Beijing, with Pyongyang as another Chinese satellite. That approach would play well in South Korean politics and also grant Seoul a greater say in what happens to or in North Korea than would otherwise be the case. Meanwhile, Russia could then add its leverage to a U.S. plan to engage North Korea directly within the Six-Party framework, as China and others have recommended. Then it might be possible to resume negotiations with North Korea under conditions acceptable to the other parties and with the promise of an expanded direct U.S. engagement that is essential to any lasting peace process. This program might also make the Six-Party process a real rather than fictitious vehicle for actually restructuring Northeast Asian security.

The second prong of this strategy relates to Russo-Japanese relations that are now at an impasse. Moscow apparently thinks it can bully Japan into accepting the postwar settlement of the Northern Territories or Kurile Islands and simultaneously induce large-scale Japanese investment in Russia, even as it insults Japanese sensitivities and refuses to reform its economy to attract more investment. Thus, Moscow plays to its domestic galleries, sends cabinet ministers to the Kurile Islands, and is even launching a development plan and military buildup there.[249] Meanwhile Japanese experts doubt that Russian energy fields there can be developed on sufficiently large a scale to fulfill Moscow's expectations of huge East Asian markets for its energy (which Japan does not now need even after its earthquake and collapse of the Fukushima reactor).[250] Japan's domestic politics also inhibit its government from relaxing its claim to all four of the Kurile Islands and certainly U.S. support for this position adds to its inflexibility.[251] But, in fact, Japan clearly has no viable answer to Russia's chauvinistic policy other than to impede investment in Russia.[252] Though Japanese businesses would like to invest in Russia if they could guarantee profitability, they will not do so until Russia changes its policies nor will the government encourage them until the territorial issues are settled.[253]

Here, too, there must be a U.S. initiative. We would probably be doing Japan a service if we persuade it to accept Putin's resurrection of Khrushchev's 1956 offer of two of the four Kurile islands as the best it will get for now because the dangers posed by a nuclear North Korea and a rising China that defends it outweigh the benefits of domestic posturing for otherwise unattainable territories.[254] Nonetheless, it is the only proposal that has any chance of succeeding of normalizing Russo-Japanese relations. It, too, would give Russia a Japanese option for investing in the RFE and completing a pipeline to the Pacific coast that would free it from excessive, even unilateral dependency on China's energy market. Meanwhile, this would reduce Japanese and U.S. fears of a Sino-Russian alliance. On the diplomatic front, these initiatives, especially if they are coordinated with our allies, would reduce China's unilateral ability to rearrange East Asia's balance of power to its benefit and help bring about a solution to two current long-lasting problems, the urgent one of finding a way to reduce the North Korean nuclear threat, while bringing North Korea into some sort of durable, legitimate regional order and second, the abnormal relationship between Russia and Japan. Absent such initiatives, Russia will almost certainly incline toward China. Indeed, there are those who claim that Russia has agreed with China's position on the disputed Diaoutyi Islands with Japan in order to gain

Chinese support for its position on the Kurile Islands, thus essentially forming a diplomatic anti-Japanese alliance.[255] This kind of bloc is precisely the threat that we have worked to prevent since 1949, and it should not be allowed to form because too many observers here are too complacent about Sino-Russian relations to notice their trend lines.

The key benefits to Russia of these moves would not just be that it no longer need rely exclusively on China as its gateway into Asian diplomacy or that it must face a potential Chinese military threat alone. Such initiatives would unlock possibilities as well for Russia to undertake successfully what is the essential precondition for its success in Asia, reinvestment, with large-scale foreign help in Siberia and the RFE. But for these U.S. and allied initiatives to succeed, Russia cannot just be a passive recipient that pockets these reforms and happily exploits them. It, too, must act to attract these initiatives and give Washington, Tokyo, and Seoul lasting reasons for believing that they will succeed. Russia must allay the heavy burden of past suspicions arousing out of its policies. To make itself worthy of partnership and to survive as a great Asian power, Russia must change its policies to keep pace with the huge changes occurring there. Obviously, the success of these initiatives is predicated upon Russia altering its present diplomatic stance over time in response to those foreign invitations. But the changes that Russia must make to gain from these offers, survive, and even flourish as an independent Asian power go deeper than that.

The changes that must occur relate to the opening up of the RFE, if not Russia, as a whole to foreign investment. The sums required to develop the RFE's blighted infrastructure and its resource base are astronomical and will not be forthcoming unless and until Russia can guarantee, as China has done since 1978, the security and profitability of foreign investment without being expropriated by local or central governing elites' capricious whims, either local or central. Essentially, this means no more Khodorkovsky cases and no more Magnitsky affairs, to cite only two of the most outstanding examples of governmental raiding of businesses in Russia. Only if Russia changes its laws and policies to ensure that property owners' rights' will be legally defended and subjected to exclusively legal processes during disputes can it attract the investments it needs to develop Russia as a whole, and the RFE in particular. We should not shy away from indicating our awareness that these changes entail profound and hopefully lasting changes in Russian politics and economics. But they are the only changes that can allow Moscow to realize its twin desires to rebuild the RFE and play a meaningful independent role in East Asia. A Russia capable of such a role would add to, rather than detract from, the regional balance there.

A Russian failure to make these moves, which we must admit is quite likely, essentially means renouncing those foreign policy objectives and the RFE becoming by default a Chinese economic colony. Indeed, as Russian leaders know and say, development is the precondition for any successful policy in Asia.[256] If Russia fails to become "a worthy economic partner" for Asia and the Pacific Rim, Deputy Prime Minister and Finance Minister Aleksei Kudrin warned that, "China and the Southeast Asian countries will steamroll Siberia and the Far East."[257] China would then also steamroll Russia in Central Asia. Similarly, Putin warned local audiences in 2000 that if Russia failed to reform, then they would end up speaking Chinese, Japanese, and Korean.[258] Russian leaders clearly know what will happen if China is the only significant investor in the RFE.

A U.S. initiative treating Russia as a serious East Asian partner, engaging in a real dialogue on security threats there, and a strong public expression of U.S. willingness to invest in the RFE in return for real guarantees of that investment, and to encourage concurrent Japanese and South Korean investment there could well elicit a favorable Russian response. But this means a fundamental change in Russian policy whose scope and far-reaching implications cannot and should not be underestimated. Therefore, it is quite possible that the Russian government will fail, as it has since 1970, to seize the opportunity in East Asia. The Russo-Chinese partnership has been largely an anti-American and anti-liberal affair since its inception.[259] It continues because it reinforces the nature of Russia's economic and political system that has led it to the brink of marginalization in Asia but which rewards its leaders handsomely. The reform of that system and of the accompanying mentalities and even pathological economic and political behaviors that accompany it are not only in the U.S. and its allies' interests. Above all, they are in the interests of Russia's people. Insofar as Asia is concerned, they are in the interest of the Russian state because otherwise only China will be interested in the RFE. Should that situation come to pass, China, but not Russia will benefit from that outcome.

These initiatives should be followed up at the relevant levels of the U.S. Army. For example, U.S. Forces Korea (USFK) and U.S. Army Pacific (USARPAC) need to continue and, if necessary, intensify their review of all possible contingencies that could occur on the Korean peninsula and do so through games, conferences, exercises, etc. both alone and with Japan and the ROK. These actions could include both civilian experts and military leaders and forces where appropriate. Beyond that and in view of the Pentagon's statement that it sees Russia as a partner in the Asia-Pacific region, it is worth considering inviting Russian civilian experts and military officials and commanders to participate where feasible in these exercises and actions.[260]

The United States should launch these initiatives because it needs help in Asia to balance a rising and increasingly aggressive China. While anti-liberalism may benefit Russia's leaders who stand to be further enriched from sell-offs of Russian material and political resources to China and the accompanying bribes, it neither benefits their successors, the Russian state, or its people. Washington should make the offer out of a deep consideration of its evolving national interest in East Asia. But should it launch these initiatives to no avail due to Russia's refusal to accept them, it will still be able, with its allies, to cope with strategic trends in East Asia. However, if Russia should fail to rise to the opportunity that now might be offered to it, Russia's interests will not be at stake. Rather, its survival as a great independent Asian power will be at risk for that issue is now on the table. Even if Moscow does not fully realize this fact, we should realize it and extend these offers to Russia for that is the most we can do. But in Asia, as elsewhere, Russia's future is in its hands.

On the other hand, in the Middle East and the Persian Gulf, there is no sign that Russia, let alone China will support further diplomatic efforts directed against

Iran. In earlier works, this author has argued strongly on behalf of an engagement strategy directed towards Iran and North Korea.[261] But Iran has contemptuously rejected that engagement when it was offered. This left the effort to enlist Russian and Chinese support against Iran. But that policy line has apparently reached the limit of its usefulness and with it any real hope for a diplomatic or purely political resolution of the problem. As Iran moves forward despite the obstacles the United States, Europe, and Israel, have put before it narrows further any hope for a nonmilitary answer to the problem. Covert action and sabotage might succeed, but again they may also fail to arrest or reverse Iran's determined program for nuclear weapons and the generation of an insurgency across the Middle East; that is, in fact, the current situation.

While the regional trends within the Northeast Asian environment require continuing resort to creative political means backed up by strong deterrent capabilities and allied unity, the conditions presently obtaining in the Gulf and Middle East increasingly suggest that such measures will only have limited success at best. It is by no means inconceivable that we could approach a situation where direct application of force to cripple, if not destroy, Iran's nuclear program, either launched by the United States or by Israel (who, as we said, cannot accept in any way a nuclear Iran bent on its destruction) becomes the only possible solution to the threat of Iranian nuclearization. But for that to be avoided, we need to induce or obtain a change in Moscow's, if not Beijing's, perception of the stakes and, more of the same, to judge from recent Russian actions and statements, is not the answer to that problem.

Therefore we need a stronger awareness of how regional dynamics affect not only Russian policy, but the overall reset policy as a whole. Only on that basis can it succeed in realizing its progenitors' hopes. These examples from both sides' domestic, foreign, and defense policies, but with emphasis here on Russian perspectives, underscore the fragility of efforts like the reset policy and the all-encompassing need on all sides for sober statecraft removed from the mythologies and realities of the Cold War or from the new mythologies of the Post-Cold War period. Putin might complain that episodes like Libya have become stable or recurring events in U.S. national security policy, but Russia, too, is a country that has been at war since 1994 and with few, if any positive, results as the tension with Georgia and the endless and failing war against insurgency in the North Caucasus show us.[262] Those conflicts, too, have lasting consequences beyond Russia's borders. Both states' progress towards international security requires more than blaming others. Instead, it requires a deeper understanding of just how interrelated the effects of crisis, policy, and war are in today's world and a more sober appreciation of the risks that even local crises, be they expected or not, can provide to the wider global environment.

ENDNOTES

1. I have addressed this issue in Stephen Blank, "The Military Dimension of Russo-Chinese Relations," Forthcoming.

2. Marcin Kaczmarski, *The Fragile 'Rest' The Balance and the Prospects for Changes in Russian-US Relations*, Warsaw, Poland: Centre for Eastern Studies, 2011, available from *www.osw.waw.pl*.

3. Andrew Monaghan, "From Lisbon to Munich: Russian Views of NATO-Russia Relations," Research Report, Washington, DC: NATO Defense College, February, 2011.

4. Moscow, *Interfax*, in English, March 23, 2011, *Open Source Center, Central Eurasia,* (Henceforth *FBIS SOV*), March 23, 2011.

5. "GOP Senators Wary of Russian Influence on European Missile Defense," *Global Security Newswire*, April 15, 2011, available from *www.nti.org*.

6. Elaine M. Grossman, "GOP Leaders Aim to Enforce Obama's Nuclear Modernization Promises," *Global Security Newswire*, May 10, 2011, available from *www.nti.org*.

7. Kaczmarski.

8. Ahmed Rashid, "How the US Intends to End the War With the Taliban," *Financial Times*, April 19, 2011, p. 9.

9. Cited in Cathy Young, "From Russia With Loathing," *New York Times*, November 21, 2008, available from *www.nytimes.com*.

10. Fedor Lukyanov, "Political No-Road Map," Moscow, Russia, *Gazeta.ru*, in Russian, April 3, 2008, *FBIS SOV*, April 3, 2008; Tsypkin cites analogous examples of this, Mikhail Tsypkin, "Russian Politics, Policy-Making and American Missile Defense," *International Affairs*, Vol. LXXXV, No. 4, 2009, pp. 784-787.

11. Fedor Lukyanov, "Russian Dilemmas in a Multipolar World," *Journal of International Affairs*, Vol. LXIII, No. 2, Spring/Summer 2010, p. 28.

12. Timofei Bordachev, "Multipolarity, Anarchy, and Security," in Ivan Krastev *et al.*, *What Does Russia Think?* London, UK: European Council on Foreign Relations, 2009, p. 63, available from *www.ecfr.eu*.

13. Kari Roberts, "Jets, Flags, and a New Cold War?" *International Journal*, Vol. LXV, No. 4, Autumn, 2010, p. 962.

14. Tsypkin, pp. 784-787.

15. *Ibid.*, pp. 784-797.

16. For a comprehensive discussion of the national security strategy, see my previous work, Stephen Blank, "No Need to Threaten Us, We Are Frightened of Ourselves: Russia's Blueprint for a Police State," in Stephen J. Blank and Richard Weitz, eds., *The Russian Military Today and Tomorrow: Essays in Memory of Mary Fitzgerald*, Carlisle, PA: Strategic Studies Institute, U.S. Army War College, 2010, pp. 19-150.

17. This does not contradict the uproar over the arms control treaty because the key issue for the Republican opposition was missile defenses, which they regard with almost theological veneration. While they are innately suspicious of Russia, it is seen as much less of a problem than Islamic terrorism or China and, as a result, gets far less attention.

18. Richard Perle, "Yes, Nukes: the Global Zero Utopia," *World Affairs*, March-April, 2011, p. 52.

19. I discussed this previously in Stephen Blank, "Russia and Nuclear Weapons," in Stephen J. Blank, ed., *Russia's Nuclear Weapons, Past, Present, and Future*, Carlisle, PA: Strategic Studies Institute, U.S. Army War College, 2011.

20. "Missile Defense Could Be the Silver Bullet, "*Moscow Times*, November 3, 2009.

21. Dmitry Suslov, "From Parity to Reasonable Sufficiency: Russian-U.S. Relations; How to Break the Vicious Circle," *Russia in Global Affairs*, Vol. VIII, No. 4, October-December 2010, pp. 51-52.

22. Igor Dzhadan, "The Doctrine of Preemptive Retaliation," Moscow, Russia, *Agentstvo Politicheskikh Novostey*, in Russian, October 21, 2009, *FBIS SOV*, October 21, 2009.

23. Sergey Karaganov, "Forward From Rest," Moscow, Russia, *Rossiyskaya Gazeta Online*, in Russian, February 17, 2011, *FBIS SOV*, February 17, 2011.

24. Pavel Felgenhauer, "The US Threat Dominates Russian Defense Spending and Foreign Policy Decisions," *Eurasian Daily Monitor*, February 10, 2011.

25. Moscow, Russia, *Interfax*, in English, January 11, 2009, *FBIS SOV*, January 11, 2009.

26. *Ibid.*; Alexander Osipovich, "Russia Tests ICBM Designed to Overcome Missile Shield," August 28, 2008, available from *www.defensenews.com*.

27. "Russia Seen Pursuing U.S. Missile Shield Tech," *Global Security Newswire*, March 24, 2011, available from *gsn.nti.org/gsn/nw_20110324_9650.php*.

28. *Ibid.*

29. Moscow, Russia, *Interfax-AVN Online*, in English, November 3, 2010, *FBIS SOV*, November 3, 2010.

30. Moscow, Russia, *Interfax-AVN Online*, in English, March 28, 2011, *FBIS SOV*, March 28, 2011.

31. Ivan Karev, "Examination By Experts," Moscow, Russia, *Voyenno-Promyshlennyi Kuryer Online*, in Russian, May 12, 2010, *FBIS SOV*, June 1, 2010; General Anatoly Kornukov (Ret.), "Test of Orbital Aircraft Leads to Militarization of Space," Moscow, Russia, *Interfax-AVN Online*, in Russian and English, April 23, 2010, *FBIS SOV*, April 23, 2010.

32. Colonel I. M. Kruptsov, "Bor'ba s Giperzvukovym Letal'nymi Apparatami (GZLA): Novaya Zadacha I Trebovaniia k Sisteme Vozdushno-Kosmicheskoi Oboroni (VKO)" ("The Struggle Against Hypersonic Flying Machines: The New Task and Demand for a System of Aero-space Defense)," *Voynnaya Mysl' (Military Thought)*, No. 1, 2011, pp. 10-17.

33. Moscow, Russia, *Interfax*, in English, December 24, 2010, *FBIS SOV*, December 24, 2010; Oleg Zegonov, "Obama's Nuclear Doctrine Opens Pandora's Box," Moscow, Russia, *www.infox.ru*, in Russian, April 6, 2010, *FBIS SOV*, April 19, 2010; Moscow, Russia, *RIA Novosti*, in Russian, April 29, 2010, *FBIS SOV*, April 29,

2010; Moscow, Russia, *Interfax-AVN Online*, in English, July 15, 2010, *FBIS SOV*, July 15, 2010.

34. Mikhail Sergeyev and Igor Naumov, "Vladimir Putin's Golden Mace, Premier prepared to Spend R20 Trillion on Rearming Army and Navy," Moscow, Russia, *Interfax-AVN Online*, in Russian, March 21, 2011, *FBIS SOV*, March 27, 2011.

35. Felgenhauer.

36. Moscow, Russia, *Interfax-AVN Online*, in English, January 26, 2011, FBIS *SOV*, and January 26, 2011, indicates Defense Minister Sedyukov's open statement that Russia is continuing to build its own missile defense system.

37. Patrick M. Morgan, *Deterrence Now*, Cambridge, UK: Cambridge University Press, 2003 p. 66.

38. Moscow, Russia, *Agentstvo Voyennykh Novostey Internet Version*, in Russian, September 10, 2008, *FBIS SOV*, September 10, 2008.

39. Moscow, Russia, *ITAR-TASS*, in English, March 22, 2010, *FBIS SOV*, March 22, 2010.

40. Andrei Uglanov, "What is Behind Washington's Ultimatum?" Moscow, Russia, *Argument Nedeli* in Russian, March 10-17, 2010, *Johnson's Russia List*, March 17, 2010.

41. "Interview with Foreign Minister Sergei Lavrov," *Rossiyskaya Gazeta*, February 21-28, 2007, available from *www.mid.ru*.

42. Arbatov, *Russia and the United States — Time To End the Strategic Deadlock*, p. 2.

43. Ryabkov, Interview, *FBIS SOV* February 25, 2010.

44. Moscow, Russia, *Interfax*, in English, February 6, 2010, *FBIS SOV*, February 6, 2010.

45. "Putin Says Russia Will build Weapons to Offset planned US Missile Defences," December 29, 2009, available from *www.guardian.co.uk/world/2009/dec/29/nuclear-weapons-russia*.

46. Moscow, Russia, *Interfax*, in English, January 21, 2011, *FBIS SOV*, January 21, 2011.

47. Moscow, Russia, *Interfax* in English, February 5, 2011, *FBIS SOV*, February 5, 2011.

48. Suslov, pp. 51-64; Mikhail Troitsky, "Containment Must Be Overcome: Long Cycles of Russian-U.S. Relations," *Russia in Global Affairs*, Vol. VII, No. 4, October-December, 2010, pp. 40-50.

49. Jacob Kipp, "Russia's Nuclear Posture and the Threat That Dare Not Speak Its Name," in Stephen J. Blank, ed., *Russia's Nuclear Weapons, Past, Present, and Future*, Carlisle, PA: Strategic Studies Institute, U.S. Army War College, 2011, forthcoming.

50. Lukyanov.

51. Andrei P. Tsygankov, "Russia's Power and Alliances in the 21st Century, *Politics*, Vol. XXX, No. 4, October, 2010, made available in manuscript from by the author.

52. Kipp, "Russia's Nuclear Posture and the Threat That Dare Not Speak Its Name."

53. "New START Enters Into Force," *Global Security Newswire*, February 7, 2011, available from *www.nti.org*.

54. On Pakistan, see Alexei Arbatov, "Terms of Engagement: WMD Proliferation and US-Russian Relations," paper prepared for the U.S. Army War College Conference "US and Russia: Post-Elections Security Challenges," Carlisle, PA, March 6-7, 2008, in Stephen J. Blank, ed., *Prospects for U.S.-Russian Security Cooperation*, Carlisle, PA: Strategic Studies Institute, U.S. Army War College, 2009, pp. 147-149.

55. Moscow, Russia, *ITAR-TASS*, in Russian, April 12, 2010, *FBIS SOV*, April 12, 2010.

56. Moscow, Russia, *Interfax-AVN Online*, in English, February 7, 2011, *FBIS SOV*, February 7, 2011; Moscow, Russia, *Interfax*, in English, August 2, 2010, *FBIS SOV*, August 2, 2010.

57. "Power Posturing—China's Tactical Nuclear Stance Comes of Age," *Jane's Intelligence Review*, August 12, 2010, available from *www4.janes.com/subscribe/jir/doc_view.jsp?K2DocKey*.

58. Steven Andreasen, Malcolm Chambers, and Isabelle Williams, *NATO and Nuclear Weapons: Is a New Consensus Possible?* London, UK: Royal United Services International, 2010, p. 9, available from *www.rusi.org*.

59. Kipp, "Russia's Nuclear Posture and the Threat That Dare Not Speak Its Name."

60. "Military Doctrine of the Russian Federation," February 5, 2010, *FBIS SOV*, February 9, 2010, available from *www.kremlin.ru*.

61. Roger McDermott, "Russian Military Doctrine Looks East," *Eurasia Daily Monitor*, February 23, 2010; Jacob Kipp, "Russia's Nuclear Posture and the Threat That Dare not Speak Its Name," Paper Presented to the Conference Strategy and Doctrine in Russian Security Policy, Washington, DC: National Defense University, Fort Lesley J. McNair, June 28, 2010.

62. Skokov.

63. Alekseev.

64. Kipp, "Russia's Nuclear Posture and the Threat That Dare not Speak Its Name"; Roger McDermott, "Russia's Conventional Armed Forces, Reform and Nuclear Posture to 2020," Paper Presented to the Conference Strategy and Doctrine in Russian Security Policy, Washington, DC: National Defense University, Fort Lesley J. McNair, June 28, 2010.

65. Dmitri Litovkin, "Ucheniia Popali v Seti," *Izvestiya*, September 28, 2009, cited in *Ibid*.

66. A. Kondrat'ev, "Nekotorye Osobennosti Realizatsii Kontseptsii Setsentricheskaia Voina' v Vooruzhennykh Silakh KNR," *Zarubezhnoe Voyennoe Obozreniye*, No. 3, March 2010, pp. 11-17, cited in *Ibid*.

67. "Ucheniia," *Zarubezhnoye Voennoye Obozreniye*, No. 8, July 31, 2009; and Aleksandr Khramchikhin, "Starye Osnovy Novoi

Doktriny," *Voyenno-Promyshlennyi Kuryer*, Bo. 6, February 17, 2010, p. 5, cited in *Ibid.*

68. Simon Saradzhyan, "The Role of China in Russia's Military Thinking," *International Relations and Security Network*, May 4, 2010, available from *www.isn.ethz.ch*; Kipp.

69. Kipp, "Russia's Nuclear Posture and the Threat That Dare not Speak Its Name"; McDermott, "Russia's Conventional Armed Forces, Reform and Nuclear Posture to 2020."

70. *Ibid.*

71. *FBIS SOV*, November 28, 2010; "Reforma Flota."

72. Mikhail Lukanin, "Navy Prepares to Defend Russian Oil," Moscow, Russia, Trud, November 24, 2010, *FBIS SOV,* November 28, 2010; "Reforma Flota: Glavnaya Ugroza na Dalnem Vostoke," *Voyennoye Obozreniye,"* December 10, 2010, available from *topwar. ru/2646-reforma-flota-glavnaya-ugroza-na-dalnem-vostoke.html.*

73. *Ibid.*

74. *Ibid.*

75. Dmitri Litovkin, "We Didn't Send Him For a Star: A Skif Flew From the North Pole to Kanin Nos," Moscow, Russia, *Izvestiya Moscow Edition* in Russian, September 13, 2006, *FBIS SOV*, September 13, 2006.

76. Moscow, Russia, *ITAR-TASS*, in English, May 5, 2008, *FBIS SOV*, May 5, 2008; Yuri Gavrilov, "Long-Range Aviation Inhabits Arctic Skies," Moscow, Russia, *Rossiyskaya Gazeta*, in Russian, May 15, 2008, *FBIS SOV*, May 15, 2008; Moscow, Russia, *IRAR-TASS*, in English, March 20, 2008, *FBIS SOV*, March 20, 2008.

77. Litovkin, "We Didn't Send Him For a Star"; Moscow, Russia, *Agentstvo Voyennykh Novostey*, April 9, 2008.

78. Wendell Minnick,"China Ramps Up Missile Threat With DF-16," March 21, 2011, available from *www.defensenews.com.*

79. Moscow, Russia, *Interfax-AVN, Online*, in Russian, December 13, 2010, *FBIS SOV,* December 13, 2010; Moscow, Russia, *RIA-Novosti,* Online, *in Russian, December 8, 2010,* FBIS *SOV*, December 8, 2010; Moscow, Russia, *ITAR-TASS*, in English, December 13, 2010, *FBIS SOV,* December 13, 2010; Moscow, Russia, *RBK Online,* December 14, 2010, *FBIS SOV,* December 14, 2010.

80. Moscow, Russia, *RIA-Novosti Online,* in Russian, December 8, 2010, *FBIS SOV,* December 8, 2010.

81. Dmitriy Litovkin, "Successors to the 'Topol' Have Appeared," Moscow, Russia, *Izvestiya Online,* in Russian, March 24, 2011, *FBIS SOV,* March 25, 2011.

82. *Ibid.*

83. *Ibid.*

84. *Ibid.*

85. Mark A Smith, *A Russian Chronology, July-September 2008*, London, UK: Conflict Studies Research Centre Advanced Research Assessments Group, 2008, p. 25, available from *www.da.mod.uk/arag.*

86. "Popovkin Details the GPV," February 25, 2011, available from *russiandefpolicy.wordpress.com/tag/vladimir-popovkin/.*

87. Yuri Gavrilov, "To Arms! First Deputy Defense Minister Vladimir Popovkin Revealed Plans to Re-equip the Army," Moscow, Russia, *Rossiyskaya Gazeta,* in Russian, July 2, 2010, available from *russiadefence.englishboard.net/t1294-interview-with-vladimir-popovkin.*

88. Moscow, Russia, *Interfax-AVN Online*, in English, March 4, 2011, *FBIS SOV,* March 4, 2011.

89. "Supreme Commander in Chief's Five Tasks. New People Are Needed to Fulfill Them," Moscow, Russia, *Nezavisimaya Gazeta Online,* in Russian, March 21, 2011, *FBIS SOV,* March 30, 2011.

90. *Ibid.*

91. President Dmitry Medvedev, cited in "Russia Ready for Meaningful Military Reform. Again. Really," available from *www.moscowsshadows.wordpress.com/2008/09/27*.

92. Moscow, Russia, *Interfax-AVN Online*, in Russian, March 24, 2011, *FBIS SOV*, March 28, 2011; Alexander Vladimirovih Muntyanu, Yuri Anatolyevich Pechatnov," Problems of Developing a Strategic Deterrence Mechanism," Moscow, Russia, *Yubileynyy Straticheskaya Stabilnost'*, in Russian, August 12, 2010, *FBIS SOV*, August 12, 2010.

93. Krasnoyarsk, available from *www.NuclearNo.rui*, in Russian, March 8, 2010, *FBIS SOV*, March 14, 2010; Moscow, Russia, *Interfax*, in Russian, January 26, 2011, *FBIS SOV*, February 3, 2011; "Remarks of Linton Brooks, National Defense University Foundation and National Defense Industrial Association Forum with Frank Miller and Linton Brooks, on Next Steps in U.S.-Russian Arms Control," Washington, DC, May 3, 2011.

94. Jacob W. Kipp, "A Long Way to Zero; Moscow Remains Reluctant to Take the Next Step," *Eurasian Daily Monitor*, February 11, 2011.

95. Moscow, Russia, *Ekho Moskvy Radio*, in Russian, February 7, 2011, *FBIS SOV*, February 8, 2011.

96. Moscow, Russia, *Interfax,* In English, March 1, 2011, *FBIS SOV*, March 1, 2011.

97. Viktor Litovkin, "War of Resolutions," Moscow, Russia, *Nezavisiamyoye Voynnoye Obozreniye,"* in Russian, December 29, 2010, *FBIS SOV*, January 6, 2011; Moscow, Russia, *Interfax*, in English, December 24, 2010, *FBIS SOV*, January 4, 2011.

98. Moscow, Russia, *Interfax*, in English, April 2, 2010, *FBIS SOV,* April 2, 2010.

99. "Arms Fitting," Moscow, Russia, *Moskovskiy Komsomolets*, in Russian, December 17, 2009," *Johnson's Russia List*, December 18, 2009.

100. "Russia Seeks to Avoid Past Mistakes at Arms Cuts Talks With US-Expert," Moscow, Russia, *Interfax-AVN*, December 23, 2009, *Johnson's s Russia List*, December 23, 2009.

101. "Interview With Aleksey Arbatov," Moscow, Russia, *Izvestiya Online*, in Russian, January 30, 2011, *FBIS SOV*, January 30, 2011.

102. Moscow, Russia, *Interfax-AVN Online*, in Russian, February 7, 2011, *FBIS SOV*, February 8, 2011.

103. Walter Pincus, "Russia's Ryabkov on U.S.-Russia Relations: 'We Can Offer Tangible Results, And We Will Do More in the Future'," *Washington Post*, January 31, 2011, available from *www.washingtonpost.com/world/russias-ryabkov-on-us-russia-relations-we-can-offer-tangible-results-and-we-will-do-more-in-the-future/2011/01/31/ABkrC6Q_story.html*.

104. Moscow, Russia, *Interfax*, in English, April 20, 2010, *FBIS SOV*, April 20, 2010.

105. Dmitry Trenin and Alexey Malashenko, *Iran: A View From Moscow*, Washington, DC: Carnegie Endowment for International Peace, 2010, pp. 20-21.

106. Alexei Arbatov, "Terms of Engagement: WMD Proliferation and U.S.-Russian Relations," paper prepared for the U.S. Army War College conference, "U.S. and Russia: Post-Elections Security Challenges, Carlisle, PA, March 6-7, 2008, in Stephen J. Blank, ed., *Prospects for US-Russian Security Cooperation*, Carlisle, PA: Strategic Studies Institute, U.S. Army War College, 2009, pp. 147-149.

107. The doctrine may be found at the president's website, "Military Doctrine of the Russian Federation," February 5, 2010, available from *www.kremlin.ru*; also available in *FBIS SOV*, February 9, 2010.

108. Federal News Service, Official Kremlin International News Broadcast, "Without a Strong Army Russia Has No Future," Interview With Defense Minister Sergei Ivanov, " February 22, 2002, Retrieved from Lexis-Nexis.

109. Dmitri Trenin, "Russia and Global Security Norms," *Washington Quarterly*, Vol. XXVII, No. 2, p. 65.

110. *RIA Novosti*, June 21, 2007.

111. "Russia Says It Wants "Equal" Involvement in Missile Shield," *Global Security Newswire,* October 25, 2010, available from *www.nti.org*.

112. Moscow, Russia, *RIA Novosti*, in Russian, March 10, 2010, *FBIS SOV*, March 10, 2010; "UN to Address Sanctions Against Iran 'soon' - Russia's Lavrov," *RIA Novosti,* April 29, 2010; Moscow, Russia, *Interfax*, in English, April 21, 2010, *FBIS SOV*, April 21, 2010.

113. As discussed earlier in Stephen Blank, ""Russia Unfazed by North Korean Nuclear Test," *Eurasia Daily Monitor*, October 13, 2006; Stephen Blank, "Russia Turns the Other Cheek on North Korean Missile Launch," *Eurasia Daily Monitor*, July 7, 2006.

114. Trenin, "Russia and Global Security Norms," pp. 65-70; Moscow, Russia, *Interfax*, December 1, 2005, *FBIS SOV*, December 1, 2005.

115. *FBIS SOV*, February 9, 2010.

116. Arbatov, pp. 147-149.

117. Mikhail Pogorely, "Prospects for Russia-US Cooperation in Preventing WMD Proliferation," Mikhail Tsypkin, ed., *Russia's Security and the War on Terrorism*, London, UK: Routledge, 2008, p. 74.

118. *Ibid.*, pp. 74-76.

119. Matthew Kroenig, *Exporting the Bomb: Technology Transfer and the Spread of Nuclear Weapons*, Ithaca, NY: Cornell University Press, 2010, pp. 148-149.

120. Arbatov, pp. 147-149.

121. *Ibid.*

122. *Ibid.*

123. Thomas E. Graham, "The Friend of My Enemy," *The National Interest*, No. 95, May-June, 2008, pp. 36-37.

124. Arbatov, pp. 147-149; Matthew Kroenig, *Beyond Optimism and Pessimism: The Differential Effects of Nuclear Proliferation*, Managing the Atom Working Paper Series Working Paper No. 2009-14, Cambridge, MA: Belfer Center, November 2009, pp. 34-35.

125. The White House, Office of the Press Secretary, Press Briefing, July 6, 2009, available from *www.whitehouse.org*.

126. Remarks by President Obama and President Medvedev at Joint Press Conference, June 24, 2010, available from *www.whitehouse.gov?the-press-office/remarks-president-obama-and-president-medvev-russia-joint-press-conference*.

127. Trenin and Malashenko.

128. "Russia Signs Decree To Ban S-300 Air Defense Missiles To Iran," September 22, 2010, available from *www.allheadlinenews.com/articles/7019988162*.

129. David Crawford, Richard Boudreaux, Joe Lauria, and Jay Solomon, " U.S. Softens Sanction Plan Against Iran,' *Wall Street Journal*, March 22, 2010, p. 4; "Insiders See Iran Sanctions Plan Watered Down," *Global Security Newswire*, March 25, 2010, available from *www.nti.org*.

130. "U.S. Fears Chinese Companies Are Breaking Iran Sanctions," *BBC News*, October 18, 2010, available from *www.bbc.co.uk/news/world-us-canada-11567740*.

131. *Ibid.*

132. Graham.

133. Arbatov, pp. 147-149; Matthew Kroenig, *Beyond Optimism and Pessimism: The Differential Effects of Nuclear Proliferation*, Managing the Atom Working Paper Series Working Paper No. 2009-14, Cambridge, MA: Belfer Center, November 2009, pp. 34-35.

134. Remarks of Ambassador Gleb A. Ivashentsov, Second Department for Asia Director, Russian Foreign Ministry," *Iran's Security Challenges and the Region*, Liechtenstein Colloquium Report, I, Liechtenstein and Princeton, NJ, 2005, p. 39.

135. *Ibid.*

136. "Nuclear Watchdog Says Iran Boosts Nuclear Work," *Reuters,* September 6, 2010.

137. Moscow, Russia, *Interfax*, in English, July 20, 2010, *FBIS SOV*, July 20, 2010; Shiraz, Khabar-e-Jonub, in Persian, July 19, 2010, FBIS *SOV*, July 27, 2010; Moscow, Russia, *Interfax*, in English, July 14, 2010, *FBIS SOV*, July 14, 2010; Moscow, Russia, *ITAR-TASS*, in English, July 14, 2010, *FBIS SOV*, July 14, 2010.

138. Vladimir Socor, "Loopholes Opening in US, EU Sanctions on Iran," *Eurasia Daily Monitor*, July 30, 2010; Vladimir Socor, "Moscow-Tehran Oil and Gas Roadmap to Circumvent Sanctions on Iran," *Eurasia Daily Monitor*, July 14, 2010.

139. Vladimir Radyuhin, "The Russian Iranian Road Map," Chennai, *The Hindu*, July 27, 2010.

140. Beirut, *Al-Manar TV Online*, in English, July 14, 2010, *FBIS SOV*, July 14, 2010; Moscow, Russia, *ITAR-TASS*, in English, July 14, 20910, *FBIS SOV*, July 14, 2010; Vladimir Radyuhin, "The Russian-Iranian Road Map," Chennai, *the Hindu Online*, in English, July 27, 2010, *FBIS SOV*, July 27, 2010;Vladimir Socor, "Moscow Uses Anti-Iran Sanctions as Bargaining Leverage on Washington," *Eurasia Daily Monitor*, July 21, 2010.

141. Remarks by President Obama and President Medvedev at Joint Press Conference, June 24, 2010.

142. Moscow, Russia, *RIA Novosti*, in Russian, March 10, 2010, *FBIS SOV*, March 10, 2010; "UN to Address Sanctions Against Iran 'Soon' - Russia's Lavrov," *RIA Novosti*, April 29, 2010; Moscow, Russia, *Interfax*, in English, April 21, 2010, *FBIS SOV*, April 21, 2010.

143. David J. Kramer, "Resetting the U.S.-Russian Relationship: It Takes Two," *The Washington Quarterly*, Vol. XXXIII, No. 1, January, 2010, pp. 69-70.

144. "Russia Could Delay Release of U.N. Report on Iran," *Global Security Newswire*, May 13, 2011, available from *www.nti. org*.

145. Moscow, Russia, Novaya Gazeta Ponedelnik, in Russian, March 16-22, 1998, Foreign Broadcast Information Service, Arms Control, (Henceforth *FBIS TAC*) 98-076, March 17, 1998.

146. "Global Alternative: The Logical Conclusion of a Major Failure of Russian Intelligence," Moscow, Russia, in Russian, November 9, 2009, *FBIS SOV*, November 9, 2009, available from *www.forum.msk.ru*.

147. David Ignatius, "What a 'Reset' Can't Fix," *Washington Post*, July 5, 2009, available from *www.washingtonpost.com*.

148. Vladimir Socor, "Moscow Uses Anti-Iran Sanctions As Bargaining Leverage on Washington," *Eurasia Daily Monitor*, July 21, 2010.

149. *FBIS SOV*, July 29, 2010.

150. "Iran Says It Has S-300 Missiles," *Associated Press, Moscow Times*, August 5, 2010, p. 3.

151. For further information, see Stephen Blank, *New Trends in Russian Arms Sales*, Washington, DC: Jamestown Foundation, 2010.

152. Jon W. Parker, *Persian Dreams: Moscow and Tehran Since the Fall of the Shah*, Washington, DC: Potomac Books, 2009, p. xi.

153. *Ibid.*, pp. 135, 146, 307-308, for example.

154. *Ibid.* I discussed this back in 1992 in Stephen Blank, "Russia and Iran in a New Middle East," *Mediterranean Quarterly*, Vol. III, No. 4, Fall 1992, pp. 124-127.

155. Parker.

156. Igor Kryuchkov, "Japan May Replace Russia in Iranian Nuclear Crisis," *Moscow, Russia, Gazeta Online*, in Russian, February 26, 2010, *FBIS SOV*, February 26, 2010.

157. Fedor Lukyanov, "Looking Back," Moscow, Russia, *Gazeta.ru*, August 19, 2010, *FBIS SOV*, August 23, 23010; Moscow, Russia, *Interfax*, in English, August 23, 2010, *FBIS SOV*, August 23, 2010; Tehran, *IRNA*, in Persian, August 29, 2010, *FBIS SOV*, August 29, 2010; Nasser Karini, "Iran Proposes Joint Assembly of Nuclear Fuel," *Philadelphia Inquirer*, August 27, 2010; "Bushehr Is Purely Economic, Not Political Issue-Analyst," August 23, 2010, available from *www.russiatoday.com*; "Russian Pundits Ponder Consequences of Launch of Nuclear Station in Iran," *BBC Monitoring from Ekho Moskvy*, August 21, 2010; Moscow, Russia, *Interfax*, in English, August 20, 2010, *FBIS SOV*, August 20, 2010; Moscow, Russia, *RIA Novosti*, in Russian, August 23, 2010, *FBIS SOV*, August 23, 2010; "Experts Debate Possibility of Iran Attack," *Global Security Newswire*, August 18, 2010, available from *www.nti.org*; "Russia: Nuclear Plant Shows Iran's right to Peaceful Nuclear Energy," *Radio Free Europe Radio Liberty*, August 19, 2010, available from *www.rferl.org*; Open Source Center, "Stated Bushehr Opening Likely Effort to Stabilize Russia-Iran Relations," *FBIS SOV* August 18, 2010; Marie Jego "Iran Inaugurates Bushehr Its First Nuclear Plant Despite Sanctions," Paris, *LeMonde.fr*, in French, August 22, 2010, *FBIS SOV*, August 23, 2010.

158. Dmitry Medvedev, "Priority Tasks for Russian Diplomacy," *International Affairs* (Moscow), No. 5, 2010, p. 20; "Russia May Nix S-300 Sale to Iran," August 19, 2010, available from *www.upi.com*.

159. Anna Smolchenko, "Russia To Reimburse Iran Over Missile Deal," October 7, 2010, available from *www.defensenews.com*.

160. Victor Kostev, "The Great Chess Game of the Middle East, " *Asia Times Online*, August 30, 2010, quoting M.K. Bhadrakumar, available from *www.atimes.com*.

161. *Ibid.*

162. Lukyanov, *FBIS SOV*, August 23, 2010; Zvi Magen and Ephraim Azulay, "Bushehr After All," Tel-Aviv, Institute for national Security Studies, in English, August 25, 2010, *FBIS SOV*, August 25, 2010.

163. Jeffrey Mankoff, "The Road to Tehran Does Not Lead Through Moscow, Russia," New York: Council on Foreign Relations, September 12, 2009, available from *ww.cfr.org/publications/20194/road_to_tehran_does_not_lead_through_moscow.html*.

164. Moscow, Russia, *Vremya Novostey*, in Russian, September 11, 2006, *FBIS SOV*, September 11, 2006; Transcript of Russian Minister of Foreign Affairs Sergey Lavrov Interview to Turkish Media, Moscow, Russia, May 29, 2006, available from *www.mid.ru*.

165. Joseph Longa, "Then and Now: Arab Reactions to the Israeli and Iranian Nuclear Programs," *Nuclear Scholars Initiative: Project on Nuclear Issues*, Washington, DC: Center for Strategic and International Studies, 2009, pp. 36-41.

166. Riyadh, "Putin Opens Saudi-Russian Economic Forum, "*SPA*, Internet Version, February 12, 2007, FBIS *SOV,* February 12, 2007; Moscow, Russia, *Interfax*, in English, February 12, 2007, *FBIS SOV*, February 12, 2007; Moscow, Russia, *Vesti TV*, in Russian, February 12, 2007, *FBIS SOV*, February 12, 2007; Cairo, *Al-Akhbar* in Arabic, February 27, 2007, *FBIS SOV*, February 27, 2007.

167. For further information, see Stephen Blank, "Russia's Proliferation Pathways," *Strategic Insights*, January, 2009.

168. "Iran Nuclear Talks Should Cover Easing Sanctions," *Reuters*, January 20, 2011; "Russia Against Iranian Sanctions," *People's Daily Online*, January 20, 2011; "Russia has no Grounds to Suspect Iran of Seeking to Possess nuclear Weapons-Putin," *Interfax*, December 2, 2010; "Russian Diplomat Says Iranian Nuclear Programme No Cause for Concern," *Interfax* December 16, 2010; "Russia Sees No Real Nuclear threat From Iran," February 22, 2011; "Russia Sees No Alternative to Diplomatic Settlement of Iranian Nuclear Problem," *Ministry of Foreign Affairs of the Russian Federation,* available from *www.mid.ru*, February 28, 2011; Moscow, Russia, *Interfax-AVN Online*, in English, February 28, 2011, *FBIS SOV*, February 28, 2011; Moscow, Russia, *Interfax-AVN Online*, in English, March 10, 2011, *FBIS SOV*, March 10, 2011; Moscow, Russia, *Interfax,* in English, January 25, 2011, *FBIS SOV*, January 25, 2011; Moscow, Russia, *Interfax*, in English February 5, 2011, *FBIS SOV*, February 5, 2011; Moscow, Russia, *Interfax-AVN Online,* in English, February 3, 2011, *FBIS SOV*, February 3, 2011.

169. Moscow, Russia, *Interfax*, January 17, 2011, *FBIS SOV*, January 18, 2011; "'Iran nearing nuclear bombs' Russia warns," *BBC News*, July 12, 2010; Ilya Arkhipov and Henry Meyer, Russian President Medvedev Says Iran Nuclear Stance `Unreasonably Tough'," *Bloomberg*, December 22, 2010.

170. "Russia Seeks New Strategy For Iran Talks," *Global Security Newswire*, February 7, 2011, available from *www.nti.org*.

171. Boris Yunanov, "Weapons Without Linkages, Russia Will Not Support New Sanctions Against Iran," Moscow, Russia, *Vremya Novostey*, in Russian, July 15, 2009, *FBIS SOV*, July 15, 2009.

172. Andrew Osborn, "North and South Korea On the Brink of War, Russian Diplomat Warns," *telegraph.co.uk*, September 24, 2010, available from *www.telegraph.co.uk/news/worldnews/asia/northkorea/8020972/North-and-South-Korea-on-the-brink-of-war-Russian-diplomat-warns.html*.

173. Sunny Lee, "China Proposes Seoul Lead Nuclear Talks," *Asia Times Online*, April 15, 2011, available from *www.atimes.com*.

174. Moscow, Russia, *Interfax*, in Russian, May 6, 2011, *FBIS SOV*, May 6, 2011.

175. Balbina Hwang; Michel O'Hanlon, "Defense Issues and Asia's Security Architecture," Michael J. Green and Bates Gill, eds., *Asia's New Multilateralism: Cooperation, Competition, and the Search for Community*, New York: Columbia University Press, 2009, p. 281.

176 . Niklas Swanstrom, "Artillery Exchange on the Korean Peninsula," *Institute for Security and Development*, Policy Brief, No. 44, November 23, 2010, available from *www.isdp.eu*.

177. Kim Se-Jeong, "Japanese Media Allege NK Preparing Nuke Test," *Korea Times*, November 17, 2010, available from *www.koreatimes.co.kr/www/news/nation/2010/11/113_76532.html*.

178. "South Korea Vows Retaliation Against Any Further Attack," *Reuters*, November 29, 2010.

179. Siegfried S. Hecker, "A Return Trip to North Korea's Yongbyon Nuclear Complex," Stanford, CA: Center for International Security and Cooperation, Stanford University, November 24, 2010, available from *iis-db.stanford.edu/pubs/23035/Yongbyonreport.pdf.*

180. "South Korea Vows Retaliation Against Any Further Attack."

181. "Not Waiving, Perhaps Drowning," *The Economist: Briefing: North Korea,* May 29, 2010, pp. 23-25; Rudiger Frank, Currency *Reform and Orthodox Socialism in North Korea,* Northeast Asia Peace and Security Network (NAPSNET), Policy Forum Online, December 3, 2009; "N. Korea Backtracks as Currency Reform Spells Riots," *Chosun Ilbo, English Edition*, December 15, 2009, available from *english,chosun.com/site/data/html_dir/2009/12/15/2009121400361.html*; Captain Jonathan Stafford, USA, "Finding America's Role in a collapsed North Korean State," *Military Review*, January-February, 2008, p. 98; "N. Korea's Currency Reform "a Bid To Cement Power," *The Chosun Ilbo English Edition*, December 2, 2009; available from *english.chosun.com/site/daa/html_dir/2009/12/02/20091202200656.html.*

182. "CIA Chief Panetta Says North Korea's Kim Preparing Succession"; Sanger and Shanker.

183. "South Korea Vows Retaliation Against Any Further Attack."

184. E.g., Sue Pleming, "Gates Says Kim Jong-Il's Son Seeks Military 'Stripes'," *Reuters.com*, August 13, 2010.

185. Sangsoo Lee and Christopher O'Hara, "Yeonpyeong on Fire and Enriched Uranium," Stockholm, Sweden: Institute for Security and Development, Policy Brief, No. 45, November 26, 2010, available from *www.isdp.eu.*

186. Daniel A. Pinkston, *The North Korean Ballistic Missile Program*, Carlisle, PA: Strategic Studies Institute, U.S. Army War College, 2008, p. 57.

187. William J. Broad, James Glantz, and David E. Sanger, "Iran Fortifies Its Arsenal With the Aid of North Korea," *New York Times*, November 29, 2010, available from *www.nytimes.com*.

188. Yongho Kim and Myungchul Kim, "North Korea's Risk-Taking vis-à-vis the U.S. Coercion," *Korean Journal of Defense Analysis,* Vol. XIX No. 44, Winter, 2007, pp. 81-82.

189. "North Korea, China in 'Consensus' on Crisis," *Global Security Newswire*, December 9, 2010, available from *www.nti.org*.

190. Evans J. R. Revere, "The North Korea Nuclear Problem: Sailing Into Uncharted Waters," *American Foreign Policy Interests,*" No. 32, 2010, pp. 183-184.

191. Moscow, Russia, *Ekho Moskvy News Agency*, in Russian, May 20, 2010, *FBIS SOV*, May 20, 2010.

192. Sangsoo Lee and O'Hara.

193. "U.S., Allies Remain Opposed to Nuclear Talks With North Korea," *Global Security Newswire*, December 7, 2010, available from *www.nti.org*.

194. For a study of Russian policy in Korea, see Stephen Blank, "Russia and the Six-Party Process in Korea," Korea Economic Institute, ed., *Tomorrow's Northeast Asia*, Washington, DC, Vol. XXI, 2011, pp. 207-226.

195. Andrei Lankov, "The North Korean Issue: What Can Be Done?" Nicole Finnemann and Korea Economic Institute, eds., *Navigating Turbulence in Northeast Asia: The Future of the U.S.-ROK Alliance,* Washington, DC: 2010, pp. 80-85.

196. O'Hanlon, p. 281.

197. Ralph A. Cossa, "The Sino–U.S. Relationship: Respecting Each Other's Core Interests," *American Foreign Policy Interests*, Vol. XXXII, No. 5, 2010, pp. 272-273.

198. Georgy Toloraya, "Russia and the North Korean Knot," 2010, available from *www.japanfocus.org/georgy-toloraya-3345*.

199. Georgy Toloraya, "The New Korean Cold War and the Possibility of Thaw," available from *www.japanfocus.org/georgy-toloraya-3258*.

200. Revere, pp. 183-184.

201. "North Korea Says No Plans To Abandon Nuclear Weapons," *RIA Novosti*, Northeast Asian Peace and Security Network (NAPSNET), April 21, 2010; "US Says Won't Accept Nuclear N. Korea," *Agence France Presse*, *NAPSNET*, April 21, 2010; "North Korea Must Rejoin Nuke Talks to Escape Sanctions, U.S. Envoy Says," *Global Security Newswire*, January 14, 2010, available from *www.nti.org*; "No End to Korea War Until North Scraps Arms: China," *Reuters*, October 17, 2007.

202. John Gerard Ruggie, ed., *Multilateralism Matters: the Theory and Praxis of an Institutional Form*, New York: Columbia University Press, 1993.

203. Gilbert Rozman, "U.S. Strategic Thinking on the Japanese-South Korean historical Dispute," Gilbert Rozman, ed., *U.S. Leadership, History, and Bilateral Relations in Northeast Asia*, New York and Cambridge, MA: Cambridge University Press, 2010, p. 151.

204. Michael Wesley, "Asia-Pacific Institutions," William T, Tow, ed., *Security Relations in the Asia-Pacific: A Regional-Global Nexus?* New York and Cambridge, MA: Cambridge University Press, 2009, pp. 49-66.

205. Gilbert Rozman, *Northeast Asia's Stunted Regionalism: Bilateral Distrust in the Shadow of Globalization*, New York and Cambridge, MA: Cambridge University Press, 2004; Gilbert Rozman, *Strategic Thinking about the Korean Nuclear Crisis: Four Parties Caught between North Korea and the United States (Strategic Thought in Northeast Asia)*, New York: Palgrave Macmillan, 2nd Ed., 2010; Michael J. Green and Bates Gill, eds., *Asia's New Multilateralism: Cooperation, Competition, and the Search for Community*, New York: Columbia University Press, 2009.

206. "DPRK Top Leader Kim Jong-Il Hopes for Early Resumption of Six-Party Talks, *Xinhua*, in Chinese, August 30, 2010,

Open Source Center, *Foreign Broadcast Information Service, China*, (Henceforth *FBIS CHI*), August 30, 2010.

207. "U.S., Allies Remain Opposed to Nuclear Talks With North Korea."

208. "South Korea Vows Retaliation Against Any Further Attack," *Reuters*, November 29, 2010.

209. Hecker, "A Return Trip to North Korea's Yongbyon Nuclear Complex."

210. "South Korea Vows Retaliation Against Any Further Attack."

211. Julian Borger, "South Korea Considers return of US tactical nuclear weapons," November 22, 2010, available from *www. guardian.co.uk*; "S. Korea Not Mulling Return of U.S. Tactical Nuclear Weapons: Gov't," Yonhap News Agency, February 28, 2011, available from *english.yonhapnews.co.kr/northkorea/2011/02/28/62/ 0401000000AEN20110228007400315F.HTML; Hwang Doo-Hyong*, "Rep. Chung calls for redeployment of tactical nukes to S. Korea," Yonhap News Agency, March 29, 2011, available from *english. yonhapnews.co.kr/national/2011/03/30/52/0301000000AEN20110330 000400315F.HTML*.

212. Dan De Luce, "US Weighs New Options Against North Korea: Gates," June 5, 2010, available from *www.yahoo.com*; Glenn Kessler, "Pyongyang Tests U.S. 'Patience'," *Washington Post*, May 27, 2010, p. 12.

213. Yu Bin, "China-Russia Relations: Reset under Medvedev: Zapad-Politik and Vostok," *Comparative Connections*, Vol. XII, No. 2, July 15, 2010.

214. Hyung-A Kim, "Re-Igniting the Cold War in Asia," *East Asia forum*, July 31, 2010, available from *www.eastasiaforum. org/2010/07/31/re-igniting-the-cold-war-in-asia/*.

215. *Ibid.*

216. Seoul, Korea, *Hankoryeh Online,* in English, July 27, 2010, *FBIS SOV,* July 27 2010; Seoul, Korea, *Joongang Daily Online,* in English, July 28, 2010, *FBIS SOV,* July 28, 2010; Seoul, Korea, *Yonhap,* in English, August 4, 2010, *FBIS SOV,* August 4, 2010.

217. M. Nikolaev, "The Asia-Pacific Region and Russia's National Security," *International Affairs* (Moscow, Russia), Vol. LVI, No. 3, 2010, pp. 68-69.

218. Moscow, Russia, *Interfax,* in Russian, September 24, 2007, *Open Source Center Foreign Broadcast Information Service Central Eurasia,* (Henceforth *FBIS SOV*), September 24, 2007.

219. *Ibid.,* pp. 71-77.

220. Address by H.E. Mr. Gleb A. Ivashentsov, Ambassador of Russia to the Republic of Korea at the 5th Jeju Peace Forum, Jeju, South Korea, August 13, 2009, available from *www.russian-embassy.org/Press20090813_chej.htm.*

221. Jacob W. Kipp, "Moscow Seeks Room to Maneuver As Crisis on the Korean Peninsula Intensifies," *Eurasia Daily Monitor,* June 18, 2010; Moscow, Russia, *Interfax,* in English, May 20, 2010, FBIS *SOV,* May 20, 2010; Moscow, Russia, *Ekho Moskvy Radio,* in Russian, May 20, 2010, *FBIS SOV,* May 20, 2010; Moscow, Russia, *Interfax-AVN Online,* in Russian, June 8, 2010, *FBIS SOV,* June 8, 2010; Moscow, Russia, *ITAR-TASS,* in English, June 4, 2010, *FBIS SOV,* June 4, 2010; Moscow, Russia, *Interfax,* in English, June 2, 2010, *FBIS SOV,* June 2, 2010; Seoul, Korea, *The Korea Times Online,* in English, June 7, 2010, *FBIS SOV,* June 7, 2010.

222. Lowell Dittmer, "The China Factor in Japanese-Russian Relations," *International Symposium, 2003: Talking Papers,* Organizing Committee for International Symposium, 2003, p. 39.

223. Freedman, pp. 22-35, Iver B. Neumann, "Russia as a Great Power," Jakob Hedenskog, Vilhelm Konnander, Bertil Nygren, Ingmar Oldberg, and Christer Pursainen, eds., *Russia as a Great Power: Dimensions of Security Under Putin,* London, UK: Routledge, 2005, pp. 13-28.

224. Moscow, Russia, *ITAR-TASS*, in Russian, February 13, 2007, *FBIS SOV* February 13, 2007.

225. *Ibid.*

226. Jae-Nam Ko, "Review of Korea-Russia Summit Talks and Future Prospects," *Korea and World Affairs*, Vol. XXXII, No. 4, Winter, 2008, p. 442.

227. *Ibid.*

228. Joseph Ferguson, "U.S.-Russia Relations: Weathering the Storm," *Comparative Connections*, April, 2008.

229. *Stenograma Vystupleniya I Otvetov Ministra Inostrannykh Del Rossii S.V. Lavrova Na Voprosy SMI v Khode Sovmestsnoi Press-Konferentsiii Po Itogam Peregovorov s Ministrom Inostrannykh Del Yaponii K. Okadoi, Moscow, Russia, 28 Dekabr'ya 2009 Goda,* December 28, 2009, available from *www.mid.ru/brp_4.nsf/0/A4B0E5CB-D7934B02C325769A004DD828.*

230. Georgy Toloraya, "Russian Policy in Korea in a Time of Change," *Korean Journal of Defense Analysis*, Vol. XXI, No. 1, 2009, pp. 67-84.

231. Jun Kee Baek, "Medvedev's Russia, a "Revisionist Power' Or an 'Architect of a new World Order"? The Evolution of Ideational Factors and Its Cases," *Korean Journal of Defense Analysis*, Vol. XXI, No. 4, December, 2009, pp. 477-481; Moscow, Russia, *Interfax-AVN Online*, in English, December 17, 2009, *FBIS SOV*, December 17, 2009; CEP20091223950097, Beijing, *Xinhua*, in English, December 23, 0837 GMT2009, *FBIS SOV*, December 23, 2009; Moscow, Russia, *Interfax*, in English, December 11, 2009, *FBIS SOV* December 11, 2009; Moscow, Russia, *ITAR-TASS*, in Russian, December 23, 2009, *FBIS SOV*, December 23, 2009.

232. Paradorn Rangismaporn, "Russian Perceptions and Policies in a Multipolar East Asia Under Yeltsin and Putin," *International Relations of the Asia-Pacific*, Vol. IX, No. 1, 2009, pp. 230-234; Toloraya, "Russian Policy in Korea in a Time of Change," pp. 77-79.

233. *Ibid*, p. 79.

234. Moscow, Russia, *ITAR-TASS*, in English, December 18, 2009, *FBIS SOV*, December 18, 2009.

235. CEP20091223950184, Moscow, Russia, *ITAR-TASS*, in English. December 23, 2009 1325 GMT, *FBIS SOV*, December 23, 2009.

236. "Russia Deploys S-400 Air Defense Systems in Far East," *RIA Novosti*, August 26, 2009, available from *en.rian.ru/mlitary_news/20090826/155930246.html*.

237. CEP20091223950194, Moscow, Russia, *ITAR-TASS*, in English, 1339 GMT, December 23, 2009, *FBIS SOV*, December 23, 2009.

238. Cheon Seongwheun, "Changing Dynamics of US Extended Nuclear Deterrence on the Korean Peninsula," *Pacific Focus*, Vol. XXVI, No. 1, April 2011, pp. 57-58.

239. As stated at the Korea Economic Institute conference, October 22, 2010, American University, Washington, DC.

240. This proposal is further outlined in Stephen Blank, "The End of Russian Power in Asia?" Forthcoming in *Orbis*.

241. Thus the Vostok-2010 exercise postulated as its operating premises, U.S.-Japanese-South Korean and Chinese attacks against Russia.

242. Akira Iriye, *After Imperialism: The Search for a New Order in the Far East 1921-1931*, New York: Atheneum, 1965.

243. Robert Dallek, *Franklin D. Roosevelt and American Foreign Policy, 1932-1945: With a New Afterword*, New York: Oxford University Press, 1995, pp. 75-81; Jonathan Haslam, *The Soviet Union and the Threat from the East: Moscow, Russia, Tokyo and the Prelude to the Pacific War: 1933-41 Vol. 1 (Studies in Soviet History & Society)*, New York: Palgrave Macmillan, 1992.

244. David M. Glantz, *August Storm: The Soviet 1945 Strategic Offensive in Manchuria*, Ann Arbor, MI: University of Michigan Library, 1984, pp. 9-43.

245. David Kerr, "The Sino-Russian Partnership and U.S. Policy Toward North Korea, "From Hegemony to Concert in Northeast Asia," *International Studies Quarterly*, Vol. XXXXIX, No.3, September, 2005, pp. 411-437; Constantine Menges, *China the Gathering Threat*, Bill Gertz, Foreword, Nashville, TN: Nelson Current, 2005; Robert Jervis, "U.S. Grand Strategy: Mission Impossible," *Naval War College Review*, Summer 1998, pp. 22-36; Richard K. Betts, "Power, Prospects, and Priorities: Choices for Strategic Change," *Naval War College Review*, Winter 1997, pp. 9-22; John C. Gannon, "Intelligence Challenges Through 2015," available from *odci.gov/cia/publicaffairs/speeches/gannon_speech_05022000.htmls*.

246. Kipp, "Russia's Nuclear Posture and the Threat That Dare Not Speak Its Name."

247. Chairman of the Joint Chiefs of Staff Admiral Michael G. Mullen, *The National Military Strategy of the United States: Redefining America's Military Leadership*, Washington, DC, 2011, p. 13; Sunny Lee, "Russia Emerging from the Cold," *Asia Times Online*, February 11, 2011, available from *www.atimes.com*.

248. "New U.S. National Military Strategy: The United States Sees Russia As an Asian Partner," *RIA Novosti*, February 10, 2011, cited in *Johnson's Russia List*, February 10, 2011.

249. Moscow, Russia, *ITAR-TASS*, in Russian, February 4, 2011, *FBIS SOV*, February 4, 2011; "Dmitry Medvedev Discussed Economic Development and Security in the Kuril Islands With Ministries of Defense and Regional Development," *President of Russia*, February 9, 2011, available from *www.kremlin.ru*.

250. Paul J. Saunders, *Russia's Role in Asian Security: a U.S.-Japan Dialogue*, Washington, DC: The Nixon Center, 2010, pp. 19-21; Shoichi Itoh, "Russia's Energy Diplomacy Toward the Asia-Pacific: Is Moscow's Ambition Dashed?" Tabatra Shinichiro, ed., *Energy and Environment in Slavic Eurasia*, Hokkaido, Japan: Slavic Research Center, 2008, pp. 33-67.

251. "U.S. Pledges Support For Japan In Stand-Off With Russia Over Kuril," *RTT News*, November 1, 2010, available from *www.rttnews.com/Content/GeneralNews.aspx?Id=1465028&SM=1.*

252. Tokyo, Japan, *JIJI Press*, in English, February 4, 2011, *FBIS SOV*, February 4, 2011.

253. Moscow, Russia, *ITAR-TASS*, in English, October 26, 2009, *FBIS SOV*, October 26, 2009; Moscow, Russia, *Interfax*, in English, October 22, 2009, *FBIS SOV*, October 22, 2009; Tokyo, *Nikkei Telecom*, in English, October 17, 2009, *FBIS SOV*, October 17, 2009; Moscow, Russia, *ITAR-TASS*, in English, August 14, 2009, FBIS SOV, August 14, 2009; Moscow, Russia, *ITAR-TASS*, in English, September 16, 2009, *FBIS SOV*, September 16, 2009; Moscow, Russia, *Interfax*, in English, December 28, 2009, *FBIS SOV*, December 28, 2009.

254. "Kuril Islands Dispute Between Russia and Japan," *BBC News*, November 1, 2010, available from *www.bbc.co.uk/news/world-asia-pacific-11664434.*

255. "Russia Notified China Prior to Medvedev Visit to Kunashiri Island," Vienna, Austria, *UIN Hatsu Konfidensharu*, in Japanese, December 31, 2010, *FBIS SOV*, January 31, 2011; "China-Russia 'Tie-up' Tests Japan Over Territorial Disputes," *Japan Today*, available from *www.japantoday.com/category/commentary/view/china-russia-tie-up-tests-japan-over-territorial-disputes.*

256. Sergei Lavrov "The Rise of Asia and the Eastern Vector of Russia's Foreign Policy," *Russia in Global Affairs*, Vol. 4, No. 3, July-September, 2006, pp. 70, 77.

257. Moscow, Russia, *Interfax*, Presidential Bulletin, in English, August 21, 2001, *FBIS SOV*, August 21, 2001, "Asia and the Russian Far East: The Dream of Economic Integration," *AsiaInt Special Reports*, November, 2002, pp. 3-6, available from *www.Asiaint.com.*

258. See *www.president.kremlin.ru/events/50.html*, cited in Aleksandr' Lukin, "Russia's Image of China and Russian-Chinese Relations," Washington, DC: Brookings Institution Center for Northeast Asia Policy Studies, 2001, p. 13, available from *www.brookings.edu/fp/cnaps/papers/lukinwp_01.pdf.*

259. "Yeltsin Okays Russian Foreign Policy Concept," *Current Digest of the Post-Soviet Press* (Henceforth *CDPP*), Vol. XLV, No. 17, May 26, 1993, p. 15; Yuri S. Tsyganov, "Russia and China: What is in the Pipeline," in Gennady Chufrin, ed., *Russia and Asia: The Emerging Security Agenda*, Oxford, UK: Oxford University Press for SIPRI, 1999, pp. 301-303.

260. Mullen, p. 13; Sunny Lee, "Russia Emerging from the Cold."

261. As discussed earlier in Stephen Blank, "Prospects for Russo-American Cooperation in Halting Nuclear Proliferation," Stephen J. Blank, ed., *Prospects for U.S.-Russian Security Cooperation*, Carlisle, PA: Strategic Studies Institute, U.S. Army War College, 2009, pp. 169-284.

262. See Stephen Blank, "Georgia: The War Russia Lost," *Military Review*, November-December, 2008, pp. 39-46.

www.ingramcontent.com/pod-product-compliance
Lightning Source LLC
Chambersburg PA
CBHW081326310526

45789CB00018B/2442

9781501055027